The Natural History
of
Southern Africa

The Natural History
of
Southern Africa

Text by David Bristow

Photographs by Gerald Cubitt

STRUIK

Struik Publishers
an operating division of The Struik Group (Pty) Ltd

Struik House
Oswald Pirow Street
Foreshore, Cape Town

Reg. No. 80/02842/07

First Published 1988

EDITOR: Ellis Pender
DESIGN AND TYPOGRAPHY: Neville Poulter
MAP: Institute for Cartographic Analysis, University of Stellenbosch

Typesetting and reproduction by Hirt & Carter (Pty) Ltd, Cape Town
Printed and bound by Printpak Books, Cape

ISBN 0 86977 737 8 (Eng DJ ed)
ISBN 0 86977 847 1 (Eng PLC ed)

Contents

Acknowledgements

It is not often that a writer gets the chance to tackle a book of this scope; I must first thank Peter Borchert at Struik for initiating the project, for overseeing the work and for his creative judgement.

Also at Struik, Ellis Pender who meticulously edited my sometimes meandering script.

It was a pleasure working with creative professionals, designer Neville Poulter and photographer Gerald Cubitt, with whom I shared a close working relationship to produce this book.

At UCT I was lucky to benefit from advice given by Dr Richard Cowling on the Arid West, Dr Mike Meadows on biogeography, Professor Eugene Moll on fynbos ecology, Mandy Lombaard of the Zoology Dept, who led me into the sands of the Namib Desert, but especially Professor John Grindley, a true naturalist.

As always, my friend and climbing colleague, naturalist and scientist Dr Bob Scholes shared his highly valued advice and ecological insights.

Finally to Tracey Hawthorne, who once again waited for me to complete my 'adventures' - and then married me.

David Bristow

Half-title page: *Only in southern Africa are the continent's dwindling rhino populations assured of survival. These massive animals are prime targets for poachers as their horns fetch high prices on international markets: in North Yemen they are prized as dagger handles, and in the Orient as a powdered aphrodisiac. The black rhino, photographed here in Zululand's Umfolozi Game Reserve, is regarded as an endangered species.*

Title spread: *Caterpillar Pan in Zimbabwe's Hwange National Park is a favourite congregating spot for elephants and buffaloes. The park's elephant culling programme is controversial, but not without benefit to the local inhabitants, to whom the resultant meat is sold cheaply. The tusks and hides are also sold to help finance the running of the park.*

Pages 4-5: *As evening draws in hippo schools become restless before moving onto land to graze. In a display of open aggression, two sparring hippos disturb the tranquillity of sunset over the Letaba River in the Kruger National Park. In this protected environment, adult hippos have no natural enemies, although rival bulls are known to engage in ritual combat during mating seasons.*

Pages 6-7: *Impala move across the Zambezi River floodplain in the Chikwenya region, where seasonal flooding encourages an abundance of tasty green shoots for these and other herbivores.*

Left: *A female leopard in the Kalahari Gemsbok National Park, South Africa.*

The Tides of Nature

THE FIRST PRINCIPLE OF ECOLOGY, which states that everything in nature is related, is now a widely accepted premise, but few people other than scientists and a small band of well-informed laymen appreciate the complexity of these relationships. Mathematicians using powerful computer programs have tried and failed to model the interactions within even the most basic ecosystems. This realization anticipates the second basic principle of ecology, which contends that you cannot change only one thing in nature, as a change to one component has ripple effects throughout an environment.

These relationships and interactions are linked in an intricate lattice that exists in the four dimensions of space and time, and perhaps even a fifth dimension whereby the collective workings of the natural world transcend the sum of its parts, where all the living and non-living things on earth and in its atmosphere behave like an independent macro-organism. The atmosphere is its lungs, the oceans and rivers are its arteries and kidneys, it has a liquid interior and a plastic skin called its mantle, which is covered in places with dense mats of dark growth while in others it is bare and pale. It is mobile, it responds to both internal and external stimuli, and it has a finite life-cycle. Perhaps it even has a controlling intelligence, which some people call Nature and others call God, while some might contend that with the arrival of mankind, the earth evolved its own consciousness.

Ecology, the study of the earth's natural systems, is derived from the Greek word 'oikos', which means home and 'logos' meaning study - the study of our home, planet Earth. Ecologists have likened earth to a space capsule with limited area and resources, with we as the astronauts cruising through the cosmos, knowing little about whence we came and even less about our destination. We cannot alter our course, and we must rely on those resources we have to hand to allow us to survive the journey. Some of these resources are renewable, like plants and animals which use energy and nutrients to reproduce themselves, while others, like metals and coal, are not renewable within the human time scale. Still others, like our atmosphere and topsoil, are renewable over hundreds of years, but we have the ability (and the desire, it would seem) to destroy them faster than they can be replaced.

The best known example of these interactions is that demonstrated by Rachel Carson in her book 'Silent Spring'. She detailed how the spraying of DDT caused an accumulation of this poison in the food-chain. The original aim was to kill only crop-eating insects in the fields, but the DDT washed into streams and rivers and then accumulated in lakes. Small fish ingested non-lethal amounts of the 'wonder' chemical, let us say one part of DDT to ten million parts of body mass. A large fish might eat a hundred smaller fish in a year and then it would have a DDT concentration of one part in 100 000

Left: *The struggle of life is primarily a struggle for food and water: on the shores of Lake Kariba a fish eagle drops its meal while a saddle-billed stork forages at the water's edge. In the background a pair of impalas take to their heels. Like most herbivores they are at their most vulnerable when drinking and will take fright at the slightest suspicious movement.*

in its body, a near-lethal amount. A fish-eating bird then consumes a hundred large fish in a year to accumulate one part of the chemical in 1 000 parts of body mass, which is more than enough to kill it, or at least to render its eggs infertile.

In southern Africa a similar chain of events followed the closure of St Lucia estuary mouth in 1969. A high rate of evaporation and reduced flow of fresh water into the estuary caused by the high water demands of the farmers upriver, resulted in salinity levels increasing from an average of 35 parts of salt to a thousand parts of water, to over 110 parts per thousand. The crocodiles could not submerge to feed; fish died in great numbers and so insects like midges and mosquitoes proliferated. This meant a large food supply for spiders, whose webs festooned the large trees surrounding Lake St Lucia in drapes of silken filament so dense that thick branches broke off. The decay of dead animals in the water led to a great supply of detritus and shellfish were poisoned by a particular type of plankton bloom known as 'red tide'.

Geographers divide the world into physical units, such as continents, countries and provinces; plant geographers divide it into floral kingdoms and floristic regions, domains and sectors, centres of endemism and communities. Ecologists are most comfortable with habitat and biome divisions, which describe not only a physical area, but also the processes at work in those areas. The levels of ecological organisation begin with the *organism*, say a cow. Cows will be found in *communities*, which could be a dairy herd. After this comes the *niche* occupied by a cow, which includes the paddock, the grass, water supply, its daily rhythms and reproductive and other behaviour. Each niche occurs within a *habitat*, which, in this case, is the dairy farm, and the farm will fall within an *ecosystem*, perhaps the eastern Cape sour grasslands. Finally the various ecosystems will fall within *biomes*, in this case the Savanna Biome.

Within the biosphere the biome is the broadest ecological unit, extending over a large geographical area and distinguished by a fauna and climax flora, geology, soils and climate, interacting as a partially closed system. There are seven biomes in southern Africa (Fynbos, Forest, Savanna, Grassland, Desert, Succulent Karoo and Nama-Karoo), and within each of these there are various main subdivisions and a few debatable ones.

For instance, the Desert Biome, Succulent Karoo and Nama-Karoo are sometimes grouped together under a general biome heading of Arid Zone. The Grassland Biome encompasses an Afro-alpine subdivision which is characterized by the fynbos heaths that are found in the Maluti and Drakensberg mountains above an altitude of approximately 2 000 metres. In turn the true grasslands are surrounded by the Savanna and Nama-Karoo Biomes, where boundaries are blurred by the uncertain status of climax communities and by the changes wrought by man. The Forest Biome includes the Afro-montane, subtropical lowland and tropical lowland forest ecosystems; the Afro-montane forests, while all having the same basic tree species, include the small relict forests of the Cape Fold mountains and the Escarpment as well as the Tsitsikamma/Knysna forests. The Savanna Biome is divided into two main components: the moist eastern savanna and the dry Kalahari savanna, each of which occupy over 30 per cent of the sub-continent.

But while biomes are useful ecological definitions, some major ecosystems of the region transcend their physical boundaries, or are not included in them. Freshwater wetlands are the most obvious example of this, where a river may flow through any number of biomes from source to sea. The coastal margin is neither biome nor ecosystem, and yet it is a distinct ribbon around the entire region, and a vital interface between land and sea. The drainage lines that are the life-giving linear oases of the Namib are not included in the

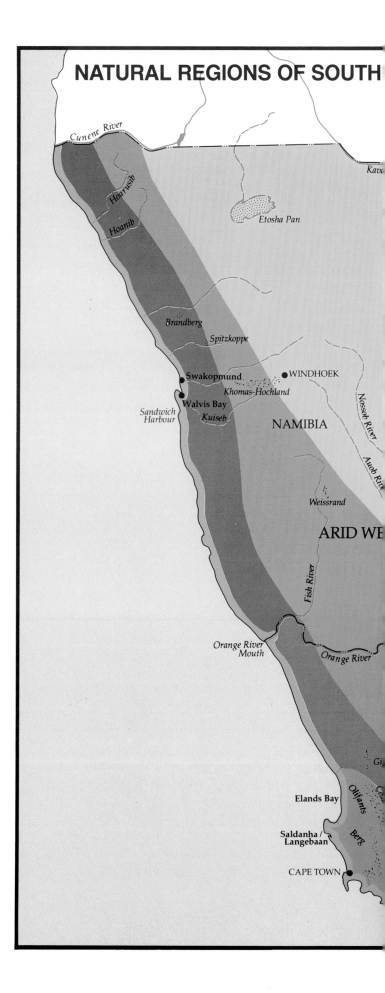

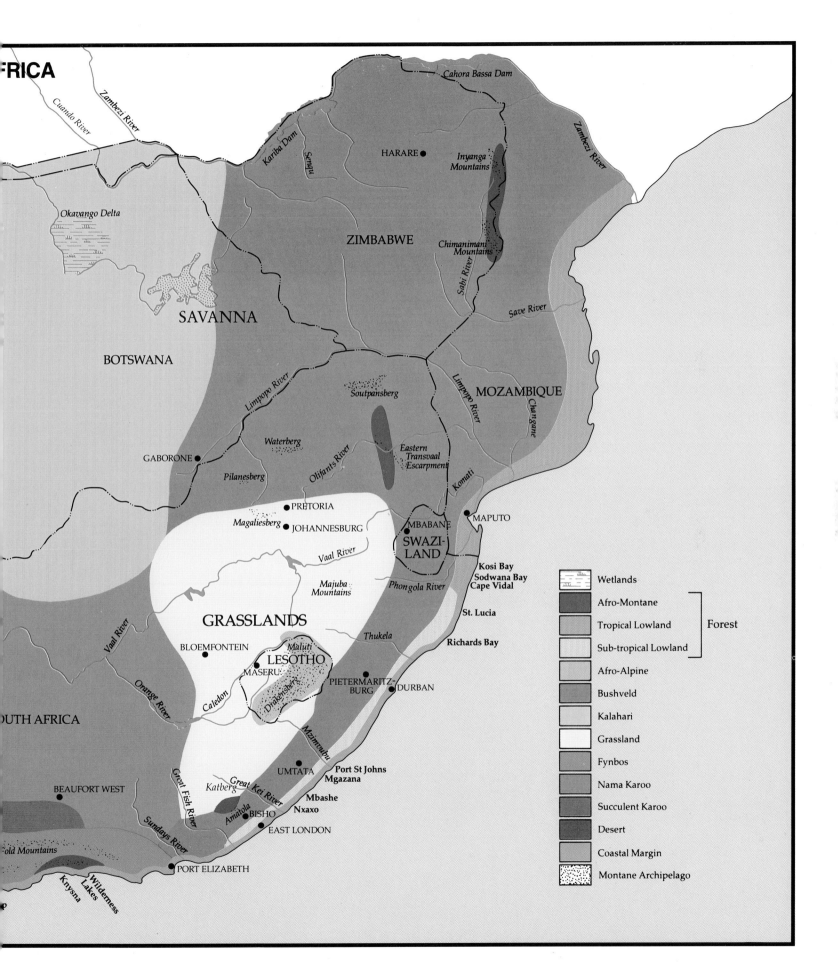

FRICA

Cuando River
Zambezi River

Cahora Bassa Dam

Kariba Dam
Sengu

HARARE ●

Inyanga Mountains

Okavango Delta

ZIMBABWE

Chimanimani Mountains

Siabi River

SAVANNA

Save River

BOTSWANA

Limpopo River

Soutpansberg

MOZAMBIQUE

Limpopo River

Changane

Waterberg

GABORONE ●

Olifants River

Eastern Transvaal Escarpment

Pilanesberg

Komati

● PRETORIA

Magaliesberg ● JOHANNESBURG

MBABANE

● MAPUTO

SWAZI-LAND

Vaal River

Kosi Bay
Sodwana Bay
Cape Vidal

Majuba Mountains

Phongola River

St. Lucia

GRASSLANDS

Thukela

Richards Bay

Vaal River

BLOEMFONTEIN ●

Maluti

LESOTHO

MASERU ●

● PIETERMARITZ-BURG ● DURBAN

Drakensberg

UTH AFRICA

Orange River

Caledon

Mzimvubu

BEAUFORT WEST ●

Great Fish River

Katberg

Great Kei River

UMTATA ●

Port St Johns
Mgazana

Mbashe

Amatola ● BISHO

Nxaxo

● EAST LONDON

Sundays River

old Mountains

Wilderness Lakes

Knysna

● PORT ELIZABETH

	Legend	
	Wetlands	
	Afro-Montane	
	Tropical Lowland	Forest
	Sub-tropical Lowland	
	Afro-Alpine	
	Bushveld	
	Kalahari	
	Grassland	
	Fynbos	
	Nama Karoo	
	Succulent Karoo	
	Desert	
	Coastal Margin	
	Montane Archipelago	

definition of the Desert Biome, as they have a higher moisture level, and are fingers of savanna and Karoo ecosystems that stretch into the desert. Scientific definitions do not always suit a general description of nature, so this book combines a number of biogeographical divisions that best describe the natural history of southern Africa.

Other examples of ecosystems having been shifted from one biome to another are the great pans of northern Botswana and Namibia. Although Makgadikgadi and Nxai pans fall within the Savanna Biome, they are really grasslands where trees have been excluded by seasonal flooding and exceptionally saline soils, and so they are included in the Grassland chapter. Likewise, Etosha Pan falls on the boundary of the Savanna and Nama-Karoo Biomes, but as dryness is its all-pervading characteristic it has been included in the Arid West chapter. The Afro-montane region of the Forest Biome does not adequately describe the sub-continent's extensive mountain chains, and so the mountains have been afforded their own chapter.

In order to understand and control his environment, man needs first to define it, but these definitions seldom do justice to nature's complex existence. The best example in southern Africa where biological definitions fall short of reflecting the actual state that exists is in the eastern Cape. Ecologists refer to this as a 'tension zone', where the Fynbos, Forest, Grassland, Savanna and Karoo Biomes all meet, advancing and retreating as conditions change. At different seasons and in different years the area around Grahamstown can resemble either a lush English country scene or a bleak Karoo landscape. Man has further complicated the natural dynamics of the area; the diaries of 1820 Settlers tell of lush grasslands around Salem that reminded them of English parks. After 150 years

of burning and overgrazing that area is now covered by aloes and sweet-thorn bushes that herald the advance of arid Karoo conditions.

To understand the natural history of southern Africa, it is necessary to note the effects of important past events, such as ice ages, volcanic activity, continental movements and the raising and lowering of sea levels, as well as events in the shorter term, such as fluctuations in wind and sea currents and flood and drought cycles. Man has sought constantly to understand the natural forces and processes that dictate the formation of life, the forms and functions of the land and living organisms and the movements of astral bodies. The similarities in structure between atoms and molecules and those of solar systems and galaxies is perhaps the most obvious example of the connection between the microscopic world and that of the cosmos. The shape of the larger coastal bays of the western and eastern Cape are all determined by a mathematical formula called a logarithmic spiral; this is the same formula that describes the inward spiralling arc of an abalone shell, a paper nautilus or a fossilized ammonite mollusc shell.

Left: Polystictus sanguineus, *one of many colourful fungi found in the temperate, evergreen Tsitsikamma forests. The cycle of nature is an endless flow of nutrients through the system. Trees grow in soil; fungi decompose trees and are eaten by small antelope or insect larva; the animal's faeces, in turn, will enrich the soil, returning to it those nutrients essential for the growth of the trees.*
Below: *Lion in the Kalahari Gemsbok National Park, South Africa.*

Freshwater Wetlands

MUCH OF SOUTHERN AFRICA'S NATURAL HERITAGE has been disturbed by human activities over the years and some ecosystems, such as the Fynbos Biome, even to the point of being threatened. There is now great concern for the plight of the whales and rhinos, the forests and the fynbos, but in truth we can live without fynbos, even though we would be physically and spiritually poorer for it. At the same time, little public attention has been given to the most threatened and abused of all our natural environments - the freshwater systems. The mountains are still wild, natural environments where pure mountain streams gush down forested kloofs, yielding high quality water to the farms and towns below. Regrettably, once such infant rivers reach the plains, and often well before, it is only a matter of time before they are irreparably harmed by man's rural and urban activities.

The Cape Town metropolis, for example, is graced by numerous streams rising on Table Mountain or the Cape Flats, which provided fresh water to the sailors and colonists of the past. Today few of these streams could be called graceful, as they have been canalized and polluted with industrial and domestic wastes. While it is true that they teem with more life than any natural river, it is only a few species of worms and bacteria that thrive on the oxygen-starved, highly eutrophic conditions of these torpid drains. Some of these organisms are pathogens, which pose health problems for the shanty-dwellers and squatters of greater Cape Town, who use and abuse its rivers. One third of the world's population doesn't have access to fresh drinking water and the World Health Organization believes that 80 per cent of all sickness in the Third World is attributable to contaminated water supplies.

Concerned limnologists are now pointing out that, because of a general lack of regard for our rivers, lakes and vleis, they are becoming less and less natural. This is due not only to vital water supply projects impounding rivers and changing their physical and chemical properties, but also because vleis are drained, swamps and pans filled in, while rivers and lakes are used for waste disposal. Farmers, whose existence depends on their natural water supplies, are perhaps most guilty in this regard. They allow their stock to overgraze the wetlands' protective edges, they fill in swamps and vleis to increase arable land and plough the river banks.

Rain water collects in vleis, in swamps and in underground springs which hold excess water and release it into streams slowly throughout the year. In its normal, youthful, mature and old stages from source to sea, a river will have a finely balanced ecosystem of fauna and flora that keeps it clean and healthy. Unfortunately, through human interference, few such rivers exist in southern Africa, and in so many cases we are left with murky dams and foetid mires.

Vleis are important areas for birdlife but they play a far subtler hydrological role of flood attenuation by absorbing rain and

---

Left: *Floodplains are a vital part of river systems. Annual floods deposit rich alluvial soils. With the subsidence of the water, these bring forth a flush of juicy new plant growth. Dwindling pools remain, where birds such as these yellow-billed storks on the Zambezi River, feed on fish, frogs, insects and small crustaceans.*

Below: *The plunging water of this seasonal fall in the Du Toit's Kloof Mountains is chemically pure and virtually free of sediments and organic nutrients. Along its course, however, the flow will slow and begin to gather nutrients to support a growing web of living organisms, but it will also pick up more and more silt from the erosion of the surrounding countryside - and pollutants.*

Right: *The wattled crane (Grus carunculata) is one of many birds that depend on wetlands for feeding and breeding. This graceful 1,5-metre-tall bird is Africa's largest crane and one of its most endangered, the South African breeding population having been reduced to about 100 pairs from the estimated 500 a century and a half ago. The crane family Gruidae has the highest proportion of critically endangered species, which is indicative of the reliance of all its species on wetlands and the destruction of this habitat worldwide. Wattled cranes build their matted nests in swamps, surrounded by water moats, in highland vleis of the Great Escarpment, central Zimbabwe and the Okavango and Caprivi wetlands, feeding on insects, frogs, small reptiles and aquatic plants.*

Far right: *Large freshwater waders are perhaps the most conspicuous birds in southern Africa. Grey herons, for instance, are found everywhere but in the heart of the Namib Desert. Like egrets, they nest in noisy heronries.*

flood waters like sponges. Natal sugar and timber farmers fill them in and then wonder why floods do so much damage to their lands and why the streams flow less vigorously than they once did. If springs and vleis are the sources, like hearts controlling the blood flow to the biogeographical body, then rivers are its arteries. To restrict their flow is like contracting collective thrombosis, canalizing is a hardening of the arteries and polluting them is poisoning ourselves.

Wetlands act as natural sediment traps where the nutrients encourage the copious growth of reeds, sedges and floating lilies. These plants act as filters to purify the streams that flow out of them. African jacanas hop across the outstretched palms of the floating lily leaves and matted vegetation, from which practice is derived their common name of lilytrotter. Extraordinarily long toes prevent the birds from sinking as they trot around and they fly low over the water with quick but irregular wingbeats, trailing their long toes behind them. Jacanas can swim well and dive for small molluscs and crustaceans and they peck at seeds and insects as they shuffle across the floating dance floors on vleis and swamps.

The Thukela River rises as a chilly and pure stream from a seepage 'sponge' on the slopes of Mont-aux-Sources. About one kilometre from its source on the summit plateau of the Drakensberg, it plunges in three giant leaps over the massive Amphitheatre wall.

The falls crash into a boulder-cluttered chute and then cascade through a forested gorge where a deep incision has been cut into the softer sandstone at the base of the basalt mountains. The water here is rich in oxygen from its tumblings over falls and rapids, racing with youthful exuberance. Like newly fallen rain water it has a high percentage of dissolved oxygen but it is virtually free of silt, which is why mountain water tastes so good.

Pure mountain water is good for drinking but cannot sustain much life. No large plants can grow in the river's upper reaches because of the low nutrient content of the water and the Thukela's abrasive action, nor many algae because little light reaches through the sylvan umbrella of the forest to aid photosynthesis. All the life here consists of insects and micro-organisms that are able to withstand the high water velocity. Most common are insect larvae which creep under rocks, burrow into the stream bed, or crouch low within the boundary layer on the bottom where the flow is slowed down by friction. Leaves from forest trees float down and settle on the surface of these pools, where they become waterlogged and sink to form a leaf mosaic on the bottom. Here they are colonized by bacteria and fungi and these are in turn consumed by tiny snails and molluscs that cling to the undersides of rocks.

Where the Thukela emerges from the gorge the valley floor widens a little and here it loses much of its energy. Medium-sized

boulders that have been rolled down from the gorge are deposited in a braided pattern near the gate of the Royal Natal National Park. From here the Thukela flows through the foothills, is swelled by numerous tributaries and flows out across the Natal Midlands as a stately, mature river. Trees still grow along its banks but more sunlight reaches the water, which now flows less swiftly and forms quieter pools and backwaters where plants can take root.

The main inhabitants here are still insects, but their numbers and diversity have increased. A new food-web is evident here, with live green plant material at the base of the trophic pyramid rather than detritus, although fallen leaves still form a large part of the nutrient pool. Less stressful conditions, warmer water and more food allow the animals in the middle reaches of the river to grow faster and generally larger than in the gorge. Dragonflies and damsel-flies alight on reed stems that overhang the stream and giant water bugs hunt tiny fish and even small frogs in the water, injecting dissolving enzymes into their prey and sucking out the liquidized animals, leaving behind only the crumpled skins. Bugs like *Lethocerus cordofanus* can grow up to 10 centimetres long on this protein-rich diet.

The Vaal River rises on the watery plateau near Chrissiemeer in the eastern Transvaal but it never has the youthful energy of a mountain stream, or even that of a strongly flowing middle-sized river, as its entire course is run across the fairly even surface of the interior plateau, where it supplies most the water needs of the Pretoria-Witwatersrand-Vereniging industrial complex. The warm and sluggish water encourages blooms of plankton which form the basis of food-chains in the old river.

The tall fluitjiesriet (*Phragmites* sp.) make a place for red bishop birds (*Euplectes orix*) to build their nests and perform their frenetic courting rituals in spring. The vivid scarlet and black plumage of the male bird makes it resemble a fat bumble bee as it darts about the reeds. Wild willow trees (*Salix mucronata*) and the larger, more common, but alien *Salix babylonica* are often the only trees that grow in the areas through which the Vaal River passes. They drop their leaves into the river, supplementing food-chains, and they provide important shade for animals and nesting for birds. Egrets and grey herons nest in the large willow trees that overhang the banks and frequent the shallows where they pluck fish from the water, crabs from the muddy bed and frogs, spiders or small reptiles from the banks.

Slow-flowing rivers deposit more than they erode, so their channels and valleys are shallow. When strong seasonal rains cause the rivers to overflow their banks, they inundate large areas of the surrounding countryside and spread fine silt across the land. The water dries up slowly, forming seasonal pans and sometimes permanent wetlands such as are found along the upper reaches of the Phongola and Mkuze in northern Zululand. Waterfowl in their thousands, such as white-faced whistling ducks, and other wetland birds are always found in great abundance at Nsumu Pan, a permanent wetland on the Mkuze River floodplain. Here they are nourished by the storehouse that is replenished each year when the river floods. The high biomass production of the floodplains supports a chain of trophic abundance, from guinea-fowl and warthog to herds of impala that come down to drink and feed.

T·H·E O·K·A·V·A·N·G·O

The Okavango River is fed by clear mountain streams which rise in central Angola and then flow southwards and eastwards into a vast basin whose focus is northern Botswana. The river wanders over the Kalahari's deep sands, searching in vain for the sea. Soon after crossing the Caprivi Strip the river finds a course between two geological faults, known as the Panhandle, where it weaves to and fro through a 50-kilometre stretch of partly submerged, dense papyrus growth. Crocodiles breed on the Panhandle's sandbars, as do the attractive African skimmers that glide over the channels during low light hours or when the moon is bright.

After running the Panhandle course the river reaches another fault perpendicular to its course, where it fans out at the tip of an inland delta extending over 15 000 square kilometres. But, like all the wetlands of the Kalahari, the delta is but a thin sliver of water that lies on a 3 000-metre-deep cushion of sand, and one small tremor from an under-lying fault could drastically change its form overnight.

The Okavango is a flood-driven ecosystem where once a year the rains that fall in its upper catchment reach the delta, filling out its channels and drowning much of the uncertain land. The channels flow between embankments of flood-deposited sands which form a cone of sediment in the Kalhari's low-lying centre. Year by year the bottoms of the channels are lifted higher than that of the surrounding wetland. Periodically the floodwater, which arrives some time in June or July, finds some channels finally raised too high to sustain its flow; it chooses lower paths, and so new channels will be born.

The pure, chilled water of the delta always surprises new visitors, who expect warm and swampy conditions, but the oligotrophic water is well filtered by the Panhandle's dense reed-beds. The sitatunga antelope (*Tragelaphus spekei*) spends most of its life in these reeds, where it feeds on young shoots

Left: *Ruler of the waterways - an African fish eagle strikes a majestic pose on its* Hyphaene *palm perch. The cry of these birds evokes the spirit of all that is still wild in southern Africa.*

Right: *Although little bee-eaters like to huddle close together at night, by day they are solitary hunters, hawking insects from vantage points along the waterways.*

Below: *The Okavango Delta is the largest and most beautiful of a series of wetlands that lie trapped in the Kalahari Basin. It is the last remaining permanent wetland of an ancient lake that once filled much of the Kalahari Basin and was the largest lake known to have ever existed. The geological faults that forced Lake Makgadikgadi's feeder channels to follow new drainage lines to the north, are the same ones that now determine the Okavango's deltoid structure.*

and rests during the heat of the day on platforms of broken stems and mats of debris caught within them. These antelope have long, splayed hooves and they can bound through deep water or swim across deep lagoons. When alarmed they bound through the reeds or dive into the water, and there they stay submerged with only their nostrils protruding.

At dusk the drums of baYei fishermen and the few remaining river Bushmen beat a frenzied rhythm which is absorbed by the descending darkness and fills its ominous immensity. Night, flecked with stars, finally settles like a Bushman's *kaross*, and then the secretive sitatunga leaves its watery seclusion and, although lions are prowling, ventures onto small islands where giant wild fig and mahogany trees grow alongside stately *Hyphaene* palms.

When camp fires finally die out around midnight, the drawn-out bark of the sitatungas can be heard cutting through the darkness. The deep grunting of lions is heard too, as they venture from island to island, hunting the antelope that sleep lightly and nervously. A rising howl floats down the winding channels, ending in a chilling, high-pitched yelp, signalling to all that the spotted hyaenas are hungry too.

Sitatunga avoid the wide channels that hippopotamuses forge through the reeds, for that is where crocodiles lie in ambush. Although crocodiles have a more fearsome reputation, hippos are aggressively territorial. The males, or females with young, will overturn boats which come too close and kill the passengers, while on land they will charge anyone they think has crossed their boundaries - their land territories are pearshaped, bulging out from the point of entry. They are notorious for emerging from the water at dusk to trample on campfires and campers alike.

Hippos play an important role in wetland ecosytems, dredging channels and forging corridors through the rank riparian vegetation. Without their bulldozing abilities channels would clog and the water flow would be cut off. They feed only at night when they graze the dry land grasses, often cropping them like lawns. The hot daytime is spent partly submerged, largely to avoid the attentions of biting flies that plague them on the land. They defecate in the water, thereby transferring nutrients from the terrestrial to the aquatic ecosystem.

The Okavango is, more then anything else, a place of birds, from the little bee-eaters to giant waders such as the saddle-billed stork and goliath heron. Most conspicuous and regal is that haunting serenader of the wild African wetlands, the fish eagle (*Haliaeetus vocifer*). By day they rule the Okavango's waterways, snatching fish from the water or stealing them from other creatures. They perch on tall trees beside the channels and lagoons, waiting for the tell-tale ripples of fish breaking the surface and then they slide forward and stretch out their broad wings. As it approaches the epicentre of the ripples, the eagle extends it legs down and forward, talons at the ready. A splash, desperate thrashing and then with slow and powerful strokes the great bird lifts itself, a tiger-fish or barbel dangling in its grasp.

Below: *African skimmers* Rynchops flavirostris *are intra-African migrants which flock on the sandbanks of the Panhandle like terns on a beach. They are extremely wary birds and when disturbed they rise gracefully and then turn in arabesques before settling again. While fishing they glide across the papyrus and phragmites reeds that line the channels, holding their pied, scimitar-shaped wings high and back like their close relatives the terns. They skim low over the surface, with the laterally flattened bill cleaving the water like a blade. The bill is a remarkable structure in which the longer, lower mandible protrudes. When it touches something edible,* the beak snaps shut and the prey, usually a small fish, is held firmly in the bright red mandibles.

Right: *Eggs are a favourite meal of the water monitor, or leguaan, and these marauding lizards are always on the lookout for an unguarded nest of a crocodile or bird.*

Far right: *The deep, resonating hoots of a Pel's fishing owl add a dramatic tone to the Okavango's night music; a duet between a breeding pair sounds like a sonorous horn section.*

Right below: *The chiming ring of the painted reed-frog dominates the delta's dark hours, belying the animal's diminutive size.*

The only piscivorous owl in Africa is Pel's fishing owl (*Scotopelia peli*), whose range forms a crescent along the large, permanent waterways of tropical southern Africa, from the Caprivi Strip and Okavango, along the Zambezi River and then down the Mozambique coast to Zululand. Because its fascinating activities are restricted to the late night hours, this great bird has only recently come to the attention of ornithologists and nature lovers. The owl's territories often overlap with those of fish eagles but battles are averted by the fact that the two birds 'work on different shifts', the owls hiding during the daylight hours concealed by the foliage of giant riparian trees.

Jacanas hop across the delicate water-lily leaves that lie on the Okavango's quiet lagoons, a sense of eternal serenity pervading the scene. The blooms of *Crinum* lilies and the lotus *Nymphaea caerulea* are the jewels lying encrusted in the metallic sheen of the lagoons. But this atmosphere conceals the fierce competition that takes place in the Okavango's backwaters: sitatunga lie in the papyrus and phoenix palm jungles, tiger-fish slash through the water, crocodiles lurk beneath the floating vegetable mats and hippos guard the pools. Reed-frogs wait motionless to pounce on mosquitoes and flies. Dragonflies buzz around like assault helicopters, homing in on smaller flying insects such as midges, while their predatory larvae attack other nymphs and even fingerlings in the tangled underwater forests. The fry of the African

pike, in turn, hunt for mosquito larvae that hang suspended from the water's surface like salamis from a pantry rafter. The fishing spider, *Thalassius spenceri*, grabs unsuspecting fish, even those many times its own size, and the heron hovers above, waiting for its next meal to swim by. Carpenter bees collect pollen dust from the water-lilies, and they and the hovering dragonflies and smaller

mayflies are plucked from the air by bee-eaters, those diminutive flying mannequins with their gay plumage and fanciful face markings.

In the permanent parts of the delta it is hard to distinguish the boundary between land and water, while on the floodplains there is none. Man is a transient visitor to this enchanting wilderness which is as varied and mysterious as the Garden of Eden must have been. But, just as in the first garden, man has spread his curse in the Okavango. Aeroplanes spray lethal chemicals to kill the tsetse flies, so that the country's cattle farmers can drive their cattle deeper into the fertile wetland, and diamond barons look to drain its waters to feed an industry that will last less than a hundred years. Botswana is a drier country than most in arid southern Africa and its water is therefore its most important resource.

The economic potential of the swamps is, however, not very great. Ecologists point out that man cannot hope to compete with nature's marvellous efficiency which has been cultivated over many thousands of years, let alone understand the complex interactions of a system where each reed stem and each drop of water (although water is seemingly limitless here) is held in a delicate equilibrium. Environmentalists likened it to the reflection in a pool. Try to get at it and it will disappear forever. Yet the Okavango remains largely undisturbed for us to cherish, full of mystery and primeval magnetism.

From its source in central Angola, the Zambezi River gains volume and stature on its journey across the Barotse Flats in Zambia, turning east at Caprivi until it it reaches reaches *Mosi o Thunya* - 'the smoke that thunders' which David Livingstone, in the true colonial fashion of his time, named Victoria Falls. Billowing spray soaks the lush rain forest, and when the river is in spate rainbows leap over the gorge. From the 100-metre-deep gorge below the falls the river follows the Zambezi Valley, with its wide valley floor covered by mopane woodland, to where it opens out into Lake Kariba.

The tops of dead mopane trees still reach from the lake's tranquil surface, like the claws of creatures drowned when the Zambezi was dammed 25 years ago. Since then a whole new trophic structure has emerged to utilize the water's altered state, creating new niches and new energy pathways. Between periods of fishing

in the shallows, wood ibises (*Mycteria ibis*) perch on the dead trees where they supplement their diet with insects and geckos snatched from their woody homes.

Below the dam the river follows a deep gorge until it breaks out onto the wide terraces of Mana Pools. The floodplain terraces look like parklands with lone baobabs or groves of sausage trees, mahoganies and rain trees providing food and shade for animals. On the higher terraces to the south, open *Acacia albida* woodland forms a buffer between the floodplain and the dense mopane forests beyond. The channel banks are fringed with feathery-tipped *Phragmites* reeds, geese and herons rest on the sandbanks alongside basking crocodiles, and hippos crowd together in the cobalt-blue water, breaking the surface and snorting at intervals.

During the wet season, aquatic invertebrates invade the shallows while the deeper pools are being flushed out. As the flood waters recede and the wide terraces begin to dry, the new plant growth attracts large herds of game from the higher *Brachystegia* woodlands. Fish eagles make easy meals of large fish that are trapped in drying pools. Saddle-billed storks walk slowly through the shallow water, jabbing at fish and frogs that abound on the floodplains, or stirring the mud with their feet to flush out crabs which they grab in their massive red and black bills with distinctive yellow saddles.

Previous spread: *In one way or another, all animals have to drink and at water-holes, such as that at Msinga in Zululand's Mkuzi Game Reserve, concentrations of game will be found throughout the day. Predators know this, and so do wildlife photographers, both of whom need to be patient and stealthy to 'capture' the wary animals that come to drink.*

Far left: *Crocodiles are survivors from the great age of reptiles and have succeeded where others could not, by being the lucky relative of early birds. Crocodiles lay eggs which, unlike those of amphibians, do not have to be kept moist while they incubate. The amniotic egg is nature's greatest packaging marvel. Its first appearance heralded an important new evolutionary development for animals which had crawled out of the oceans as amphibious reptiles and into the swamps of the Karoo Basin. Crocodile eggs remain viable when the temperamental African rivers dry up. But essentially these fearsome reptiles live and die in the water, bequeathing their nutrients to the wetlands.*

Left: *Weavers, like this male red bishop bird in full breeding plumage, attach their wonderful, compact nests to reeds and overhanging branches along all permanent wetlands throughout South Africa.*

Below: *This baby sitatunga antelope, born on a floating reed platform deep in the Okavango Delta, will spend much of its life in the shallow waterways of the region.*

From their first upland eagerness the rivers of the Transvaal and Natal Lowveld now slouch towards the sea, seemingly reluctant to be enfolded in the embrace of the ocean from which they were born and to which all water must eventually return. They are the haunts of a creature from an ancient dynasty, a creature far older than the rivers themselves - the Nile crocodile, the only carnivore which regularly makes meals of humans. Although crocodiles feed mainly on the large freshwater catfish (known locally as barbel or vundu) that are found in all the warm rivers of southern Africa, they will eat any fresh flesh or carrion.

They mate in the water of large rivers and up to 80 white, hard-shelled eggs are deposited in nests the female digs above the high-water mark. The eggs are vulnerable to predators during their 90-day incubation period, but the nest is guarded by the female, who leaves it only to go down to the water to drink. The biggest threat to the briefly untended crocodile nest is the monitor lizard, or water leguaan (*Varanus niloticus*) which can attain a length of two metres. They are found in all the places where crocodiles occur, and are as at home in the water as they are on land. They play an important role in controlling crocodile populations, but of course crocodiles themselves happily make a meal of these nest raiders when the opportunity presents itself.

Previous spread: *Regrettably, mankind and elephants seem incapable of peaceful co-existence and everywhere we are witnessing the twilight of Africa's greatest progeny. In all of southern Africa, Chobe is the stronghold of the elephants, but even here they are under threat because of the considerable damage they cause in the surrounding farmlands.*

Above: *Hippos may appear sluggish on land, but when disturbed they will make for the water with surprising speed - and exhibiting immense power. In the water, too, they can move with unexpected agility, as any boatman who has survived a charge will testify.*

Right: *Water lilies, such as this Crinum species, provide tasty meals for the herbivores, birds and mammals that forage among the vegetation of the wetland waterways.*

Forests

*I*MAGINE THE SURPRISE IF, WHILE SNEAKING through the gossamer embroidery of a rain forest, you came upon a massive grey form, as big as a tree but rounder, and slowly gliding away! Elephants may be the most unexpected forest residents but are more common in this habitat elsewhere in Africa than their southern African numbers would suggest. The only forest in this region that they inhabit is the Knysna/Tsitsikamma complex - and at last count there was only one, at most two, left.

While forest elephants have been shot to near extinction, one of their distant relatives survives there well enough. Forest shrews are small but voracious predators of the forest floor. They scurry through the tangled undergrowth and litter for two hours at a time, hunting for worms and insects, and then they take a quick 15-minute nap between foraging bouts; this goes on for most of the day and night. Their frenetic lifestyle requires that they consume up to 80 per cent of their body weight every day.

Forest shrews (*Myosorex* spp.) themselves may be in no immediate danger of extinction, but the habitat on which they depend may well be. The Forest Biome covers only 0,01 per cent of southern Africa, of which about 37 per cent is conserved. This seems a high proportion, but the total area conserved is below the minimum size needed to ensure the long-term survival of an ecosystem.

In tall forests there is a feeling of walking in a sylvan cathedral, where our whispers mingle with the music of streams and birdsong which swells and floats up the leaf-vaulted aisles, soft light filtering through the clerestory foliage. Massive columns of buttressed yellowwood and ironwood, Cape holly and stinkwood, Cape chestnut and wild pear are draped with a filigree of lichens and ferns, the mossy rocks and fungus-flecked ground closeting us in cool well-being.

The forests of southern Africa are like ecological islands dotted along its eastern escarpment and coastal belt, an archipelago of relict forest patches, strung out across oceans of savanna, grasslands and fynbos. During Miocene times, about 20 million years ago, a period of heavy rainfall allowed riverine and montane forest to spread out and form a near-continuous cover over most of eastern tropical Africa. Then about five million years ago, the aridity of a Pliocene ice age squeezed the forests up the mountain slopes, into sheltering kloofs and along the eastern coastline.

The vertical thrust of a forest aptly reflects its function, for in the competition for light, the trees grow tall and thrust out canopies of broad, bright green leaves high above the ground. The tall trunks are really a communication system between the soil and the canopy, designed to get the leaves to where they can use sunlight to produce food while at the same time providing them with nutrients. Green

---

Left: *The vegetation around the Matenga Falls in Swaziland is lowland riverine forest, including some bushveld species. Afro-montane and sub-tropical lowland forests once covered most of southern Africa's moister southern and eastern regions. With a progressively drying climate, over the past five million years, these forests have been forced back into relict patches, mainly along rivers and in gorges, on south-facing mountain slopes and along the coastal margin.*

chlorophyll in the leaves uses water, carbon dioxide and sunlight to produce sugar and oxygen. Large trees transpo-evaporate enormous quantities of water each day. This creates a negative pressure at the top of the tree. The suction created in the process, plus the powerful cohesive properties of water, sets a siphon in motion. The water molecules stick together to create an upward flow which carries with it nutrients from the soil, such as nitrogen and phosphorus, up through capillaries in the trunk, to help the tree to grow.

The various species of large forest trees appear very much alike and so do their leaves. This makes identifying them a frustrating activity - especially as the leaves are out of reach and out of sight, and the filtered sunlight dazzles upturned eyes (most foresters learn to identify trees from their bark). The leaves of most forest trees are broad-based and tapering (ovate), with shiny, waxy upper surfaces which act as sunscreens and for waterproofing. This convergence of structure results from the trees all having to cope with the same habitat conditions, so while forests may appear to be stable and highly resilient, their structural homogeneity makes them vulnerable to changes in the environment.

There are two broad types of forest on the sub-continent: Afromontane and sub-tropical to tropical lowland rain forest. They were probably once all linked across the region; where their ranges overlap there is still a degree of mixing between the two and structurally they are the same. Since the Pliocene epoch the two types of forest have had to contend with quite different environmental conditions, but they still share some genera and species. The critical factors determining the distribution of the two forest types are rainfall and (minimum) temperature. The actual amount of rain needed depends on the season of maximum rainfall, varying from about 600 millimetres for winter rainfall and 1 000 millimetres for summer rainfall areas.

Relicts of Afro-montane forests stretch from Newlands Forest on Table Mountain, through the gorges of the Cape Fold mountains and including the Tsitsikamma Forest, then along the Natal Drakensberg, the Eastern Transvaal Escarpment, up to the Eastern Highlands of Zimbabwe and right up into Ethiopia. As one travels along this mountain spine it is apparent how the species composition of the forests changes between the temperate south and tropical north.

Far left: *In the canopies of evergreen forests colourful butterflies flit amongst the vegetation, performing a visual symphony. Individual species are hard to identify as the insects tend to stay high above the ground or move too quickly and erratically to be seen properly. The citrus swallowtail or Christmas butterfly (Princeps demodocus) is the best known member of the family Papilionidae, appearing in forests and most of the surrounding countryside throughout the year but particularly at Christmas time.*

Left: *One of the giants of the Tsitsikamma forest, this Outeniqua yellowwood has grown from no more than a seed, nurtured by water and the soil in which it grows.*

Below: *The shy and beautiful crested guineafowl (Guttera pucherani) is easily recognizable by its curly black crest.*

The tropical and sub-tropical forests have greater variation than the Afro-montane type. In Mozambique and Zimbabwe they range from dry deciduous to moist evergreen and include fringing or riverine forest, one of the most spectacular examples of which is the rain or cloud forest which clings to the precipices around Victoria Falls. From Zululand southwards, forest composition becomes even more complex, with specialized sand, dune, swamp and fringing forest types and widespread 'undifferentiated lowland forests'. Well-known examples of this last type are the Gwaliweni Forest on the Lebombo Mountains, Ngomi and Ngoye forests in Zululand, the forests of the Natal midlands, the forests at Port Shepstone and Port St John's, and Dwesa and Manubi forests in Transkei. The Alexandria Forest in the Eastern Cape is at the southern limit of the sub-tropical flora and is a unique combination of several vegetation types.

Dwesa Forest, which spans the Mbashe and Nqabara river mouths in Transkei, is not only a particularly beautiful spot, it is also fascinating as it is not floristically related to any other Transkei or southern Natal forests, nor to the Alexandria or Tsitsikamma forests, nor to the Drakensberg forests to the east; rather, and peculiarly, it

is most closely associated with Gwaliweni Forest in northern Zululand. A suggested reason for this relates to the soil types: most forests in southern Africa are found on sandy, oligotrophic soils derived from Table Mountain Sandstones or Quaternary sands, whereas Dwesa Forest lies largely on Beaufort shales of the Karoo Supergroup. The Karoo rocks weather to nutrient-rich clay soils, as does the volcanic basalt of the Lebombo Mountains on which the Gwaliweni Forest grows.

Dwesa represents the southern limit of species such as the Natal box tree (*Buxus natalensis*) the fine-grained wood of which is prized for carving, and the northern limit of the Cape box (*Buxus macowanii*) among others. It is also the habitat of many rare and endemic trees and herbs and small creatures like the very rare frog *Natalobatrachus bonebergi*.

Undoubtedly the strangest 'forest' type in southern Africa is found in the underground forests of the Kalahari. The Barotse region seems to be the evolutionary centre of these strange, sparse shrubs like *Euclea crispa*, the blue guarri. Below ground, however, the short-lived shoots grow from massive, woody rootstocks which are all related to large forest trees or lianas. The evolution of these 'geoxylic suffrutex' plants seems to be in response to unfavourable conditions caused by seasonally waterlogged sandy soils, that are anaerobic and low in nutrients.

These conditions are typical of the low relief of the Kalahari Basin, and of *dambos*, which are seasonal pans in the Savanna Biome where the ground has not been rejuvenated by the African erosive cycle which followed the breakup of Gondwanaland, the super continent, between 100 and 85 million years ago. The sandy soils become waterlogged in the wet season and dry out in the dry sea-

Below: Polystictus sanguineus *fungi thrive in the dark, damp recesses of the temperate forests of Knysna and Tsitsikamma, where these saprophytes consume and recycle the wood of dead trees.*
Right: *The Cape dwarf chameleon is a most successful hunter, using stealth and its excellent camouflage to surprise insects. The beetle in this chameleon's mouth was dispatched with a swift flick of its sticky-tipped tongue.*

son - conditions hardly conducive to nurturing large trees. Where fire or erosion causes habitat destruction of forests and grasslands, suffrutex species often colonize the areas. The Rhodesian teak (Baikiaea plurijuga), normally a savanna genus, has recently been identified as an intermediate form between woodland and suffruticose grasslands, where it forms dwarf forests.

Forests are generally composed of three storeys: the high canopy, a smaller tree and shrub understorey and a herbaceous layer of ferns and other 'hemicryptophytes'. The leaves of the canopy transpo-evaporate and cool the lower layers in much the way that a refrigerator works; the understorey layers also 'perspire' to create a damp and refreshingly cool and shady environment. A forest releases vast amounts of vapour into the atmosphere, creating a humid microclimate, circulating water and also holding a vast store of nutrients in its plants. But its fertility is deceptive, for cut down and remove the trees and you will be left with poor, acidic soils which are easily eroded by the pounding rain, while noxious metals are brought to the surface where they form a brick-hard crust. This ground can support little agriculture and will take thousands of years to regenerate, if left alone.

To protect a forest from disturbance and help it to regenerate, the margin is vital. The fast-growing trees and shrubs which naturally fringe a forest act as a buffer by shading and protecting slow-growing seedlings and creating conditions conducive to their survival. They protect emergent trees from fire and browsing animals and, being fast growing and accessible, are favoured by rural communities for fuel and building material. If the narrow margin is destroyed it leaves the forest open to direct onslaught and also destroys its ability to spread outwards. A broken margin is like a hole in a dyke, which tends to widen as the flooding sunlight encourages weeds in the gaps at the expense of seedlings. Gaps created in a forest by tree felling and road building are even more detrimental to the forest, as they create breaks in the microclimate and allow destructive forces into the heart of the ecosystem.

But in forests there are natural grassy clearings where we suddenly stumble into dazzling sunlight, often seen dancing on a waterhole in the middle of the glade. The circular margins of low, fast-growing trees and shrubs create an ecotone between the glade and the forest; the year-round grasses provide food for bushpigs while the shrubs provide browsing for bushbuck and red duiker. Forests do not teem with large animals, for their annual output of biomass is very low and most of the green matter is held in its canopy, which favours birds, insects and primates.

Of the many hunters in a forest, none quite matches those expert marksmen of the undergrowth, chameleons. They move along branches with slow rocking movements and their skin pigment takes on the general hue of each background, making them look like swaying leaves.

misippus, for example, fools its predators by having evolved a wing pattern like that of its less tasty and poisonous model, the monarch. Even more amazingly, the four colour variations of the monarch are cunningly duplicated by the mimic species.

By far the most successful carnivores of this habitat are the ants, specifically army ants of the marauding genus *Dorylus*. Just before rain falls a mysterious trigger mechanism signals these nomadic ants to emerge from their temporary nests in awesome cohorts to scour the forest floor. Any animal, living or newly dead, that is encountered is at once set upon by a horde of ants, using their vicious jaws to slice the hapless victim into tiny pieces, which are then carried back to the nest. They move about their business with mechanical resolve, driven by the 5-centimetre-long queen which is blind, wingless, can hardly walk but is capable of producing up to four million eggs a month.

A host of lower plant forms thrive on the decay in a rain forest, plants like mosses, ferns, fungi, algae, lichens and liverworts. The most widespread and interesting of these organisms are the lichens, such as old man's beard (*Usnea* sp.) which festoons the branches of trees, or the bright yellow and orange patches found on rocks. Fungi proliferate in forests where they may be parasites, saprophytes and even predators, growing around other organisms and slowly consuming them.

In both numbers and functional importance in the ecosystem, invertebrate decomposers like worms, flies and bacteria far outweigh larger animals in the forest. As the soils on which forests grow are mostly oligotrophic and most nutrients are held in the living biomass, decay and recycling is the real source of nutrients in the sys-

Left: *Although not strictly arboreal, vervet monkeys are restricted nevertheless to forests and wooded savanna. They are omnivorous, but survive mainly on a vegetable diet, often raiding nearby croplands. They are preyed upon by leopards and forest-dwelling crowned eagles.*

Above: *All three species of duiker are shy, mainly nocturnal antelope, which inhabit areas of thick bush or forest. The largest and most common of these is the grey duiker, which is sometimes a nuisance in cultivated farmlands. The name duiker is the Afrikaans word meaning 'diver', and this describes the manner in which it disappears into the undergrowth when disturbed.*

Right: *Most of the animal life in mature forests is to be found in the high canopy, where food is plentiful. This situation favours birds, such as the purple-crested loerie, which eats both fruit and insects. It is a shy bird, but its call is rather startling, sounding similar to a defective alarm clock.*

There are numerous small insect-eating birds in rain forests, but it is the larger fruit eaters, such as parrots and loeries, that are more impressive and play an important role in the regeneration of trees. The seeds of the fruits they eat are voided over a considerable area, helping to distribute them more widely than would otherwise be possible. The heavily-casqued silver-cheeked hornbill has an enormous, sharp beak which is designed for slicing open leathery fruits and the casque probably helps to crack open hard seed pods, as well as being a mating accessory.

If our forests had more milkweed, the skies above them would be a symphony in orange, its notes the fluttering wings of monarch or milkweed butterflies. *Danaus chrysippus* contains an emetic poison, and birds which survive a meal of these butterflies will have the monarch's wing patterns deeply etched in their memories. Butterflies are among the most vivid and conspicuous forest residents, the sharp profusion of their shapes and colours highlighted against the soft backdrop of greenery. But a close look will reveal an amazing degree of similarity among many species. The tasty *Hypolimnas*

tem. When a large tree dies it is immediately set upon by a myriad of small creatures that break down the exchangeable matter and replenish the system. Death and decay are vital links in maintaining the flow of materials and energy through the ecosystem.

Below: *Like duikers, bushbuck are shy, mainly nocturnal animals which inhabit the thick bush and forests of the eastern parts of southern Africa. To the north their range extends across all of Zimbabwe and into the Okavango and Caprivi riverine forest areas. They are the prey of leopards, and occasionally pythons are known to prey upon them in the riverine bush of the Lowveld.*

Right: *Hunting spiders of the genus* Oxypodes *live in forest canopies, where they attach their egg-cases to branches or leaves. Some species are particularly attractive, and they can be seen leaping, cat-like, at flying insects or chasing their prey across the vegetation.*

Far right: *The braying calls of trumpeter hornbills can be heard along the eastern and northern fringe of the sub-continent, wherever there are tall, dense woodlands. They forage in groups for large insects and for fruit, particularly wild figs.*

Right below: *The variety of flowering plants found in equatorial rain forests is lacking in temperate and sub-tropical regions; however, orchids and other flowers, such as these mauve impatiens, can be found amongst the soft greenery of the Magoebaskloof Forest in the Eastern Transvaal.*

The Montane Archipelago

AFRO-MONTANE FORESTS FRINGE THE archipelago of mountain 'islands' stretched out along Africa's eastern flank, south of the Sahara. These highland massifs rise above the surrounding savanna and grassland 'seas' to form a habitat that is on average cooler and moister than the surrounding lowlands. In this habitat a distinct, temperate Afro-montane flora has taken hold. The plants of these mountains are all so similar, and so distinct from those of the lowlands, that they have attracted the attention of travellers from the time of the earliest botanical explorations of the continent.

Most of southern Africa's mountains form part of the Great Escarpment which embraces the sub-continent, like a necklace of varied geological beads. Each one is unique and yet all are bound by a unity that transcends even their botanical and geological connections, for mountains are places apart, where the activities of the lowlands are but a distant hum, where great birds soar grandly from their elevated eyries, and where men retreat to in meditation and in search of solitude and adventure.

From the time when Africa broke away from Gondwanaland, erosion's insatiable hunger and gravity's omnipotent force began slowly, imperceptibly, to wear away the high Gondwanan surface and to create the newer, more complex African landscape. Mountains were chiselled out of the protruding formations, or older and more resistant rocks were stripped of the surrounding ground to leave them standing aloof. The Gondwanan and African surfaces can clearly be seen in the three-tiered landscapes of the Natal Drakensberg and in the Karoo National Park above Beaufort West, where the Nuweveldberge descend for nearly 1 000 metres in steps composed of iron-hard dolerite sills to the Great Karoo plain.

While the mountains themselves represent the full spectrum of the sub-continent's geological formations, each one has its own peculiar natural features and resulting biological patterns. For instance, the Outeniqua range of the Cape Fold mountains has temperate forest clinging to its southern kloofs and lush green fynbos reaching up the southern slopes to the summit ridge and then down until it meets the succulent scrub of the Little Karoo in the rain shadow on the northern side of the range. Far across the wide Little Karoo valley the daunting Swartberg rises, the semi-desert flora of the succulent Karoo slowly giving way again to the more welcoming mountain fynbos where mist and rain are intercepted by the higher peaks, such as the massive turret of the Towerkop.

The plants which gather in the lower watercourses of the Brandberg, Namibia's highest mountains, and proliferate so unexpectedly in the higher valleys do not belong to the Afro-montane community. They are an odd mixture of dry savanna trees and desert shrubs that find a milder habitat and greater water supply here than the surrounding desert offers. The Brandberg is an isolated 'in-

---

Left: *Even in the most remote parts of South Africa, conflict with stock farmers has resulted in the almost complete eradication of large mammalian predators. Only the secretive and nocturnal leopard survives in notable numbers outside games reserves and national parks - particularly in the mountainous areas of the Cape.*

selberg', besieged by the bleak, wind-blasted expanses of the Namib Desert. The Konigstein, which rises to 2 697 metres is the highest peak in Namibia and also, surprisingly, the highest peak in southern Africa beyond the central Stormberg formations that form the Drakensberg and Lesotho mountains.

There are secret pools among the Brandberg's labyrinth of ramps and balconies. Rosy-faced lovebirds come from their nests in distant acacia trees to drink here in the evenings. They share their sundowner sips with Réppell's parrots whose yellow shoulder-flashes and blue tail-feathers mark their otherwise dull, grey plumage. The parrots spend their days in the spreading fig trees that grow in the lower ravines, scrambling among the branches like avian primates feeding on the wild fruits.

Succulent plants such as the stubby cobas trees (*Cyphostemma* sp.), grow on the rocky slopes above the gorges. These trees have pale brown bark which peels in cream-coloured flakes. Once the small yellow-green flowers fade towards mid-summer, bunches of grape-like fruits ripen from green to red, but the colouring comes from the poisonous oxalic acid they contain. On top of the massif there are five prominent peaks, and between them lie shallow bowls where grass tufts and aloes grow in gritty soil, while swamp lilies grow around the seepage areas of springs that feed the shallow pools. One delicate lily that defies the Brandberg's fierce countenance is the water-loving *Androcymbium melanthioides* which is found around small vleis below the Konigstein and the Numas Felsen.

From the Brandberg's commanding heights one can look across the pale desert landscape to the south, where the granite domes of the Spitzkoppe and Pontok Mountains rise like monuments out of the desert. The largest, Groot Spitzkop, looks like a giant fist that has punched its way through the earth's crust; smooth walls stand above a jumble of lower convex ramps and massive, rounded boulders that glow deep red in the dying sunlight. The enclosure formed by these intrusions is littered with huge granite marbles and the stone tools of the small Khoi nomads who lived under the overhangs here in times long past, when the climate was wetter, the grass more abundant and game moved across the plains that stretch wide between Namibia's few but fascinating mountain outcrops.

On the opposite side of the sub-continent the mountains are quite different, where ridge after rocky ridge of Zimbabwe's Eastern Highlands rises from a sea of tropical miombo woodland. Crests of the Chimanimani and Inyanga Mountains are far more jagged and complex than the granite domes that are typical of Zimbabwe's interior. Typical trees of this woodland are the tall and symmetrical msasa trees (*Brachystegia spieciformis*), which also are fairly common in the mountains where they assume more stunted and spread-out poses, the trunks and branches curved and twisted, resembling Clanwilliam cedar trees.

The vegetation of Zimbabwe's eastern mountains varies from grasslands which remind one of the Eastern Cape's Amatola range, to fynbos which grows on the edges of the high forests here and looks just like the Cape mountain flora, to the forests, a mixture of tropical and Afro-montane species, like the forests of the the Eastern Transvaal Escarpment. The *Philippia* bushes that grow in the open erica heaths of the sub-Alpine belt look very much like protea trees, and in fact various plants of the family Proteaceae are also found in the eastern highlands, such as the Chimanimani sugar bush (*Leucospermum saxosum*), the highveld protea (*Protea caffra*) and the silver sugar bush (*P. roupelliae*) that are widespread through the highlands from here to Transkei.

Zimbabwe's Eastern Highlands form a series of bio-geographical stepping stones between the Alpine regions of the Dra-

Left: *'The Horns' of the Wolkeberg straddle a deep fault, where hikers can peer down into the Letsitele River Valley of the Lowveld.*
Above: *The favourite habitat of rock kestrels is montane grassland, but, as their requirements are highly variable, these birds may be found in savanna and even desert areas. They eat mostly small mammals, as well as small reptiles, birds and insects.*

kensberg and the mountains of East Africa. While the geology of the Eastern Transvaal escarpment is quite different from that of the Natal Drakensberg, the escarpment forms a convenient corridor for the progression of the region's montane flora on its north-south sweep through sub-Saharan Africa. The north-eastern Transvaal escarpment is similar to the neighbouring Zimbabwe highlands, both being composed largely of quartzites and lined up along a north-south axis.

Rivers have cut deep passages through the Eastern Transvaal mountains, such as the Blyde River Canyon, where gallery forest forms high tunnels over the rivers and creeps up the shady slopes. Massive gorges are tucked away within the Escarpment's folds, cooled by forest cover and plunging waterfalls, while the ridge tops and northern aspects swelter in year-round sunshine. Some species persist only in small, isolated populations in relict forest patches or on the higher peaks. The butterfly *Charaxes marieps*, for instance, is found only on the summit of Mariepskop, a 1 944-metre peak that juts up to the east of the Three Rondavels which loom over the Blyde River Canyon. These isolated peaks are disjointed units of a former surface that has been selectively eroded away - ecological islands within the montane archipelago.

There are typically three vegetation belts in the mountains, each one determined by altitude, to an extent by latitude, as well as by the legacies left behind by past conditions. Only the highest ranges and peaks, or those of suffiently high altitude and high latitude,

will boast all three in well-defined belts. The lowest and therefore most widespread belt is called montane, and it is characterized by grassy slopes interspersed with proteaceous bushes, with various types of riverine bush in the less sheltered valleys and forest in the gorges and on shady slopes. Above the montane belt is a sub-Alpine layer, comprising sour grasses, usually *Themeda* below and a *Themeda* and *Festuca* or *Merxmuellera* community above. Low boulder scrub lines the stream-beds, while an ericaceous vegetation replaces forest in the moister, shadier enclaves. Between the fynbos and the boulder scrub, where there is enough moisture, tree ferns and cycads are common, as well as flowering plants like orchids, moraeas and red hot pokers.

Finally, on the highest areas of Lesotho and the Drakensberg,

above 2 860 metres, there is a true alpine heath where plants do not exceed one metre in height. Various helichrysums and ericas dominate the bland alpine heaths of the summits, interspersed with grasses such as *Festuca*, *Merxmuellera* and tufts of the unpalatable *Aristida*, but in spring moraea blooms and the iridescent sunbirds that flitter around the firebursts of red-hot pokers (*Kniphofia* spp.) add splashes of colour along the stream banks, while everlastings (*Helichrysum* spp.) liven up the drab, weather-stunted heaths. In southern Africa only the Amatola mountains of the eastern Cape, the high Lesotho plateau, the Drakensberg summit and a few isolated high peaks like the Kompasberg in the Sneeuberg mountains accommodate a sub-Alpine or Alpine flora.

The edge of the Drakensberg Escarpment is perhaps the most

Left above: *Until quite recently the Cape vulture was regarded as an endangered species. After as many as 15 years of intensive research on their breeding colonies, and with the establishment of vulture 'restaurants', the status of this raptor has improved. Although their range has been drastically reduced by the disappearance of wild herds, the remaining breeding colonies seem to have stabilized, and chick mortalities have decreased. They nest on north-facing cliff faces to benefit from the warmth of the sun in winter. Ironically, it is in the Cape that their numbers have been most drastically reduced.*

Left below: *Found in the mountainous areas of the Cape, the red disa is a common orchid which flowers in spring. Legend has it that this flower was the inadvertent cause of the death of Elize Meiring, the 'hex' of the Hex River Mountains. It is also the symbol of the Mountain Club of South Africa.*

Above: *The mating bond of black eagles is very strong and if undisturbed a pair will produce a brood of two fluffy white chicks (only one of which usually survives) year after year on their nests of jumbled sticks, which rest on cliff ledges. Some old nests rest as high as two and a half metres above their ledges. Black eagles are found wherever there are rock dassies, which constitute about 90 per cent of their diet.*

dramatic landscape in southern Africa, the sheer 1 500-metre wall of the Amphitheatre offering the greatest altitudinal difference on the sub-continent. Clouds break against the headland and wash over it like the sea crashing against cliffs; they swirl around the Devil's Tooth spire and the massive Sentinel tower which stand guard over the great wall. The grandeur of the Drakensberg is aptly captured in its Zulu nume of 'Quathlamba', meaning a barrier of up-turned spears. On early summer mornings the spear-like spires of the Mnweni Needles and Pinnacles, mighty Mponjwane, the Dragon's Back and the Rockeries stab through the sun-tinted clouds, washing them in shades of gold and diluted blood.

If you stand on top of the Drakensberg witnessing the splendour of dawn and you turn around, you will see no 'other side' of these mountains. The Escarpment forms an imposing retaining wall to the highland kingdom of Lesotho, a bleak and wind-whipped plateau with scattered grass tufts and boggy areas, such as the seepage area above Mnweni where the Senqu River rises, eventually finding its way to the Atlantic Ocean as the Orange River. The summit is very wet and hot in summer, thrashed by violent storms and scorched by increased ultra-violet light that penetrates the thin atmos-

Left: Sehlaba-Thebe, or 'the shield', is a unique place in the Drakensberg, as it is lower than the main Escarpment, but higher than the rest of the Little Berg plateaux. Because of this, it supports a number of endemic plant species. The many tarns are the most appealing natural features of Lesotho's only national park, which is named after this prominent peak. These tarns attract large numbers of waterfowl and other wetland birds, as well as game.

Left below: Stark skeletons of once grand trees protrude from the Cedarberg's rocky outcrops. After the cedar forests had been felled for timber, fires eliminated most of the remaining specimens of these slow-growing trees, other than those growing in the rockiest shelters.

Right: One would expect reptiles to be confined to the warmer regions of the Drakensberg, and yet the number and variety of lizards found in the Little Berg region is quite astonishing. Although the area is often covered with snow, lizards, such as this Pseudocordylus viridis, *survive comfortably on the Sehlaba-Thebe plateau.*

phere. In winter heavy snowfalls are likely to occur three or four times a year, otherwise frost coats the ground and ice petrifies the mountain streams.

The largest species of tortoise in southern Africa is the mountain tortoise, found throughout southern Africa's mountains where it lives in relative peace from predators on the lower grassy slopes. In Lesotho and Transkei, however, *Geochelone pardalis* has been hunted to extinction by local peasants. Everywhere in the wilds the newborn are vulnerable and mountain tortoise hatchlings are like walking meat pies. They frequently fall prey to southern Africa's most magnificent mountain hunter, the awesome black eagle (*Aquila verreauxii*) which soars the mountain thermals and cruises the ridge winds, gliding silently but fast to pluck small prey from the ground, pounce on sun-mesmerized dassies or knock an unsuspecting klipspringer over the cliffs.

While most raptor populations have been withered through persecution or as a result of habitat change, black eagles are still common residents in all southern African mountains. Breeding pairs delight mountaineers with the aerial acrobatics of territorial and mating displays, diving and swooping over the mountain tops, clasping talons and tumbling earthwards, their white back crosses and wing windows flashing. Black eagles display all year round over their territories and breeding pairs will always fly, perch and roost together.

The struggle for survival on the Drakensberg summit is sometimes as intense as that in the desert, especially in wintertime when there is little food available and the water is frozen. It is not so much the low temperatures that cause stresses to living organisms as the range in daily and annual temperatures, and in this regard the Drakensberg is certainly extreme. Among the creatures that brave the winters here there is a system of resource redistribution in which 'wealth' accrues to the most cunning.

At the top of this food-chain are the mountaineers who bring exotic foodstuffs into the ecosystem. Basuto bandits relieve them of warm hiking gear and staple food stuffs like coffee and sugar, as well as tobacco, boots and warm clothing. Hiking packs left in tents and caves are raided by baboons who fancy the richer fare such as patés and cheeses, strewing the packaging across the heaths. Next come the ravens and crows who squawk and squabble over the scraps like vultures around a carcass. At night little ice rats, known affectionately to mountaineers as 'wurzels' (*Otomys sloggetti*) rummage around the bottom of the food pile, sneaking into packs and nibbling at apples and biscuits.

Basuto ponies in the high valleys of Lesotho huddle together against the chilling bite of cold fronts, but the lammergeiers that nest in niches on the cliff faces are well protected against winter's harshness. Lammergeiers (*Gypaetus barbatus*), as anyone who has seen them soaring along the Drakensberg will tell you, are the rulers of the mountain skies and are the most magnificent of all raptors. The lammergeier has an outer coat of large, baggy feathers that covers a thick inner layer of down right down to its feet. When it is sleeping or in flight the bird tucks its feet into the downy layer at the base of the tail. The nests are situated on north-facing cliffs to catch morning sun in winter, when these great golden birds will stand with their 2,5-metre wingspans outstretched, soaking up the heat.

The former range of this half-eagle, half-vulture was from the Western Cape, all along the mountains of Africa, through the Middle East to the Himalayas and China. Lesotho and the Natal Drakensberg are their only remaining territories in southern Africa that offer the pastoral mountain environment they rely on, where they can find carrion and bones which they swallow whole or drop them onto rocks to expose the marrow. The lammergeier is noted in the Red Data Book on endangered species as 'rare' and is clearly threatened with extinction in southern Africa. There are thought to be about 300 of them left, but many of the nests are known to local Basotho who shoot and trap the birds - and yet the reduction of their habitat through human expansion is still the biggest threat to their survival.

Stretching out from the trio of peaks known as Thaba Ntsu, 'the mountain of lammergeiers', lies Sehlaba-Thebe - Lesotho's only national park. Its name means 'the shield' for the plateau above Bushman's Nek is higher than the rest of the Little Berg, and yet lower than the main Escarpment, creating a unique habitat where a number of endemic species are found. Among these endemic plants is the water-lily *Aponogeton ranunculiflorus* that grows in the many tarns that decorate the 10-kilometre-long shelf of sub-Alpine grasslands. It was discovered there in 1970 and subsequently dubbed 'the crown jewel of Sehlaba-Thebe'. Water birds such as black and yellow-billed duck frequent these tarns, as do blue cranes and an occasional flock of wattled and even crowned cranes.

The Cape Fold mountains are the most south-westerly out-

Above: *Klipspringers are common throughout the rocky and mountainous parts of southern Africa, but their behavioural trait of standing on prominent outcrops makes them easy targets for hunters. It is in fact a behavioural adaptation for evading predators. Unlike other antelope they do not run and hide when danger is spotted, but prefer to keep the predator in view, when they can rely on their agility in rocky terrain to escape.*

Right: *Although it is called the mountain tortoise, Geochelone pardalis is not a montane species and prefers the arid bushveld and tropical coastal plains. It is mainly herbivorous, feeding on grasses and succulents, and occasionally on small bones or carrion.*

lying refuge of the Afro-montane flora: montane trees are confined to river courses while a distinct Mountain Fynbos vegetation has established itself on the contorted parallel ranges. Witels Kloof in the Hex River Mountains is a spectacular cleft, incised deep into the middle of the most inhospitable mountains of the region. The bottom of the gorge is a place of great beauty, where trees and flowers soften the harshness of the high peaks and ridges; water as clear and fresh as liquid wind rushes over the polished boulders and forms deep, chill pools. Red disas grow on mossy banks, their brilliant red heads nodding to the rhythm of the river's melody, while on narrow ledges that line the kloof gorgeous 'painted ladies' (*Gladiolus* sp.) peer coyly down on the splendid scene.

Many mountaineers and botanists consider the Cedarberg to be the finest mountain wilderness in the Cape, if not in all of south-

ern Africa. The range is named after the Clanwilliam cedar trees (*Widdringtonia cedarbergensis*) which grew in large forests within the range's elevated valleys. A few small groves of these stately trees still stand, but most were felled to feed the growing needs of the early Cape Colony where the sweet-smelling and fine-grained wood was highly prized. Since then fires have prevented the slow-growing trees from re-establishing themselves, and even those that enjoy the protection of rock outcrops are now mostly old and dying. Gnarled forms of the once handsome trees loom from their rocky tombs, the beautiful, light-yellow wood weathered to dark grey, stark limbs clawing the air.

Some spectacular plants are confined entirely to the Cedarberg Wilderness Area, such as the flare-like capsules of the rocket protea (*Leucospermum reflexum*) that grows near the Shangri-la hamlet of Wuppertal, and the snow protea (*P. cryophila*) which grows only on the very highest peaks. Not only does this protea occur at the altitude where snow falls in winter, but its flowers actually resemble snow balls, with frosted white bracts and fluffy white flower buds. The mountain rose (*P. nana*) grows in milder valleys of the Grootwinterhoek mountains above Tulbagh, which are part of the wilderness area. As befits a wilderness area leopards are still fairly common, although rarely seen, in these mountains.

While mountain leopards have a bad reputation in the Cape because of their taste for sheep, the Cedarberg Wilderness Area has been proclaimed a leopard sanctuary, where troublesome animals that are trapped in the more southerly areas of the Western Cape have already been set free to roam this mountain vastness. Instead of sheep the leopards will be able to capture the ubiquitous baboons, rock dassies or dainty klipspringers (*Oreotragus oreotragus*) which perch on prominent outcrops, from where they can observe toiling hikers.

These small antelope have extremely coarse hair that keeps

Above left: *Frogs of the genus* Rana *are commonly found on the banks of mountain streams, where they pick insects and larvae from the surface of the water or from plants which fringe the water's edge.*
Above: *Hikers tread warily along mountain routes in case they should come across a puff-adder sunning itself on the path. In autumn these reptiles become overfed in preparation for hibernation and are sluggish from the cold. These potentially lethal snakes become so inert that they have to be prised out of the way.*
Right: *By far the most common flowering plants of the Afro-montane highlands are the gay everlastings, of which the genus* Helichrysum *is the most representative. Although this large group of plants is thought to originate in the Cape, it is equally possible that they originated from the tropics. From there, these fynbos plants have followed the mountainous spine of Africa southwards, where changing conditions allowed them to proliferate.*

them warm when snow covers the mountain slopes. Each hair is like a small, sharp quill so when leopards kill a klipspringer they grip the fur and bang the small antelope against a tree or rock until the skin tears and eventually strips away from the flesh. Klipspringer hooves are specially adapted to their rocky habitat. The hooves of a young klipspringer look like those of any other antelope, but the last joint of the foreleg is swivelled so that it walks on tip toe. As it ages the sharp tip of the hoof wears down and the klipspringer is left with cylindrical hooves. Each hoof has a hard nail-like tip with a spongy pad which affords an excellent grip; this allows the 'klippies' to leap about on cliffs that would daunt many rock climbers.

Because of their inaccessibility and their generally poor and eroded soils, discouraging agriculture, the mountains of southern Africa constitute undoubtedly the most pristine of its ecosystems. But with the advent of national hiking ways throughout most of the

region's highlands, the general popularity of outdoor recreation and the increasing pressure from rural populations, even these areas are not immune from degradation. Man and nature are one, and it is to the mountains that we must go in meditation to reassert this bond. Unfortunately, many who venture there do so disrespectfully and with scant regard for the majesty surrounding them.

In the autumn of 1988, a helicopter from a newly-built luxury hotel in the Drakensberg crashed while attempting to land guests on one of the range's hard-won peaks. No one was injured, but in local taverns it was suggested that the mountain gods had vented their displeasure at this impudent 'sacrilege'.

South Africa's great statesman and philosopher Jan Smuts encapsulated the belief of many mountaineers when he said: 'We may truly say that the highest religion is the Religion of the Mountain... the religion of joy, of the release of the soul from the things that weigh it down'.

The Bushveld

THE BUSHVELD IS THAT MYSTICAL PLACE where bleeding sunsets drip into the upturned arms of baobab trees, where the rising yelp of hyaenas cuts through the twilight, funnelled across lakes and down wide river channels, like an assegai piercing the air. This is the Africa we have come to know through heroic hunting sagas, from the pioneers like Captain Cornwallis Harris and naturalists like Frederick Courtney Selous, to legendary game rangers like Harry Wolhuter, who killed a mature lion with his pen knife. It is a place of drumbeats beating out an ancient pulse; a primal paradise that possesses the imaginations of all who know it - but the heavily armoured thorn trees, lethal serpents and merciless carnivores are there to ensure that no impurities spread through this Eden.

And what would Eden be like, without snakes to slither through the foliage or to lurk in the dense bush? Most of southern Africa's poisonous snakes are to be found in the Bushveld, including two of the most feared. The black mamba (*Dendroaspis polylepis*) is certainly dangerous and lethal, yet more myth than fact is told about its behaviour. It reaches an impressive 3,5 metres in length and is the largest venomous snake in Africa, second only to that most magnificent of all snakes, the king cobra of tropical Asia. Despite a reputation for aggressiveness, it is a shy snake that will stay holed up in old termite mounds, tree trunks or stone heaps if left undisturbed. But it is a snake with a nervous disposition and so anyone unlucky enough to get between a black mamba and its escape route will be attacked without hesitation, and, in most cases, to be bitten is to be given a death sentence. The mamba will attack rapidly and with great force, injecting large amounts of its potent neurotoxin as it bites repeatedly, aiming for the upper body and face. Luckily, black mambas are seldom seen and even less frequently encountered.

Only those who have cared to spend time watching snakes will appreciate their strange beauty, their aesthetic lines and their grace, and few snakes are more attractive than the vine snake (*Thelotornis capensis*). It has a slender body and the scales and body coloration resemble bark; even when projecting far out from a branch they will be missed and birds have been known to perch on them. This is most unfortunate for the birds as the vine snake's other name is bird snake, with obvious consequences. Like the boomslang (*Dispholidus typus*), it is back-fanged and *seldom* inflicts fatal bites on humans, which is just as well since there is no anti-venom available for its poison and anyone receiving a serious bite will slowly bleed to death.

Humans generally have a disproportionate fear of snakes, which are rarely seen and whose bites are seldom fatal (most snake bite fatalities are believed to be caused by shock). An animal which is far more obtrusive, however, is the hippopotamus. Hippos and

Left: *Giraffes go silently about the savanna's woodlands. Although a common sight at bushveld waterholes, they can exist for long periods without drinking and so are also found deep in the arid Kaokoveld. With their rubbery lips and long, prehensile tongue they are able to grasp even the thorniest acacia branches. Seemingly harmless, the giraffe can deliver a lethal kick to any predator, including the lion.*

crocodiles are responsible for more human deaths in Africa than any other creature. Hippos are territorial and aggressive and a bull will savagely attack any man, beast or boat that enters its space. They appear to dislike campfires and have been known to emerge from the riverine bush at night to stamp them out - and if any hapless campers are in the way, they too are likely to be stamped on.

While hippos seem to swallow half the view with their gaping midday yawns, crocodiles bask on sandbanks, belying their own lethal power and speed. Summertime here is eternal and in the midday heat only the screech of cicadas cracks the oppressive, sweltering canopy of the sky. Large herds of game follow seasonal migration routes, seeking out sweet grasses and water, but most predators are territorial and they must then make do with the shy, habitat-bound animals to survive. All in turn are pursued by the most cunning predator of all - man.

In the past man has been a hunter and conquerer of the wild, but today his biggest impact is as a protector, for the rangers and wardens who guard the reserves may prove to be the most vital link in maintaining the flow of energy and materials to ensure that ecosystems are kept healthy and invigorated. This is as it should be, for while the struggle for survival is the overriding mechanism of nature, it is really co-operation and the ritual avoidance of violence that determines behaviour and the survival of most animals. Most of the major game reserves in southern Africa are to be found in the Bushveld - and this is hardly surprising since the Savanna Biome (almost a synonym for Bushveld which excludes only the southeastern strip between the Escarpment and coastal plain) covers about 75 per cent of the sub-continent.

Above: *An African sunset. While the African savanna was the birthplace of man, and perhaps of all terrestrial life millions of years ago, it is here that we are witnessing the twilight of many of the world's most magnificent creatures. For, in his insatiable urge to expand his own technological kingdom, man has forsaken his fellow creatures.*
Right: *In the past wild dogs acquired the reputation of being terrible killers, but it is now recognized that they are efficient, methodical and economical hunters - surely a commendable quality in the Bushveld. They cannot hunt alone, but social bonding makes each pack an effective, deadly predatory machine.*

The Bushveld can be divided into an arid section, consisting of the Kalahari; a section of low-lying drainage systems with rich soils and dry hill slopes; and a moist, eastern thornveld and miombo section with associated poor soils. Where rainfall is high and the soils fertile the ground has largely been cleared to grow maize, sunflowers and groundnuts. The biome includes just about every stratigraphical unit of southern Africa and every main soil type, and yet by and large it is a homogeneous, flat area that hunters of old referred to as 'miles and miles of bloody Africa'.

The arid savanna has an abundance of what botanists classify as C4 grasses, those species with a low lignin content that are highly palatable and do not withdraw their nutrients into their roots when the dry season approaches, as do the less nutritious C3 grasses of the moist, eastern dystrophic areas. The grass plains of the dry west are therefore called sweetveld and are favoured by both grazing game and cattle. During years of good rains the arid savanna has a higher carrying capacity than the moist savanna, but the game has evolved nomadic habits so as not to overstay its welcome and deplete the food source during the inevitable droughts. Man, however, has managed to upset this delicate pattern of resource utilisation by entrenching himself on these marginal agricultural lands.

The Nata River, bordering the Makgadikgadi Salt Pans, lies on the edge of the central Kalahari thirstland. Here pastoralists have established permanent villages and towns and their cattle have overgrazed the sweetveld and allowed nutrient-poor desert scrub to encroach into the grasslands. Pale chanting goshawks sit in tall acacia trees, bateleurs and martial eagles soar across the plains to pluck off the spring-hares that proliferate under these conditions. It is ironic that spring-hares have now become an important food source for the cattle herders that live in these degraded parts of the Kalahari.

Up the middle of southern Africa runs an ancient trading and hunting route that was named the 'Pandamatenga' (the 'pick-up-and-carry' route) by porters of the now-famous white hunters who followed this route into the darkness of the continent. The road travels along the eastern Kalahari boundary and then veers west to pick up a series of lakes,   pans and rivers that push deep into the thirstland. Passing Makgadikgadi, Lake Xau, Lake Ngami, Nxai Pan and the expanse of the Okavango Delta, the road comes to the Chobe River before veering east again to the thundering Victoria Falls on the Zambezi River.

When Frederick Courtney Selous first saw the Chobe he wrote of 'impenetrable jungle' that lined the river and of 'stately teak forests' that stretched to the horizon. Some of this forest remains, but along the river it looks like a battlefield where only shattered trees survive. During the dry season the Chobe River is the watering place of hosts of game, including thousands of elephant, which love to bathe in the cool water and wallow in the mud shallows.

The concentration of elephants here, animals which daily drink about 150 litres of water and can consume over 250 kilograms of leaves and grass, has been building steadily over the years with disastrous consequences for the riverine woodlands. It seems that for the habitat to survive this invasion most of these elephants will have to die - either by culling or by them destroying their own food source. This is currently one of the most controversial issues of bushveld management. A principle of ecology is, 'when in doubt - do nothing', but many people nonetheless find it difficult to sit back and watch the land slowly dying.

There is no doubt that elephants have a bulldozer-like effect on the land, ring-barking marula trees, gouging out huge holes in baobabs for the moist, pulpy bark and knocking over acacias and mopane trees just to get at their leafy crowns. But many ecologists believe this to be a natural process of habitat modification rather than destruction, where the flow of energy is continually being channelled through new pathways but never lost. If elephants de-

stroy too much of their habitat they themselves will probably die off to a point where the vegetation is allowed to recover, albeit in a modified, more diverse state. After all, the idea of reducing these noble creatures to pet food is a repugnant one to most of us.

Elephants certainly are a significant vehicle of change in the bushveld, but then so is climate and geomorphology. Mound-building termites probably have an equally large impact and even tiny organisms like disease vectors can cause large-scale ecosystem changes. This happened at the turn of the century when an outbreak of the rinderpest virus killed off most of the wild and domestic ungulates in southern Africa.

The Makgadikgadi Salt Pans stretch across the central Kalahari like cowhide stretched tautly over the resouding emptiness, heatwaves beating out the rhythms of mirages and distant horizons. Once these seasonal pans were part of a prehistoric lake that covered most of Botswana, bigger than any lake on earth today. It may have been changes in climate or the upheaving earth's crust that pushed back the great rivers that fed such a lake. In the distances beyond Makgadikgadi's reach lie other, smaller pans, such as Lake Ngami, into which in generous years the Okavango Delta disgorges its ex-

Left: *A lioness gnaws the forequarter of a buffalo carcass, while a cub prefers the softer belly organs. Although lionesses account for most of the kills, the strongest members of the pride eat first, which usually means that a male has first choice.*
Above: *Repulsive and even macabre by reputation, the spotted hyaena features prominently in superstition and folklore. This arises from a misunderstanding of its fascinating, nocturnal behaviour and the awesome biting power of its jaws. Modern research has proved it to be a sensitive social animal and one of the most successful hunters of the Bushveld.*

cess water, Lake Xau fed by the Boteti River, its banks lined with magnificent trees, and Nxai Pan, all remnants of that ancient inland sea, but all life-giving oases when the rains do fall.

Many travellers and hunters of the last century rested at the copse of giant baobabs which grow on the edge of the seasonal Nxai Pan. These trees have been immortalized in the diaries of old hunters and in a famous painting by that indefatigable wanderer, Thomas Baines. Baobabs are trees of dry, hot woodlands, and nowhere

are they numerous, but they are perhaps the most conspicuous trees of the African Bushveld. Especially in the driest areas they become concentrations of life and one-tree ecosytems.

Hornbills of the genus *Tockus* (grey, red-billed, yellow-billed and crowned) make their nests in natural holes in these and other trees and once the eggs are laid, the female seals up the entrance with mud (partly provided by the male) and faeces leaving a vertical slit through which the male will feed her and her nestlings. After the eggs hatch, the female breaks out and shares the job of feeding the nestlings, which are walled up again. The fledglings finally have to hack their way out of the nest. Thick-tailed bushbabies (*Otolemur crassicandatus*) leap about the baobab branches to eat the hard but juicy fruits, while fruit-bats home in on the foul-smelling flowers and unknowingly pollinate them. Flocks of red-billed buffalo weavers (*Bubalornis niger*) build their communal nests in the high bran-

ches and thrive on the insects that gather around the fruit and flowers; boomslangs (*Dispholidus typus*) slither around the trees to find eggs and nestlings, and raptors are always nearby to catch a fat weaver or greater blue-eared starling (*Lamprotornis chalybaeus*).

Seeds of the woody fruits, sometimes called cream of tartar, are used to make a drink used for treating fevers and scurvy. Large baobabs in the north of the Kruger National Park have been aged at over 3 000 years. These trees can withstand fierce bush fires but they cannot withstand the persistent attack of elephants who gouge out and strip the thick, moist bark.

One tree that can withstand ringbarking by elephants and is found throughout the Bushveld is the marula (*Sclerocarya birrea*). The fleshy yellow fruits contain four times as much vitamin C as do oranges and they are greatly favoured by game and man alike. Elephants apparently become intoxicated from eating the fermenting plains. On the slopes there will be broad-leaved trees with low bio-mass production while below there will be fineleaved trees with greater biomass production. Soils scientists refer to a vertical soil profile, but with the catena landscape concept a horizontal profile defines a reproducible set of soil and vegetation changes. Because of the Bushveld's homogeneity, by studying a few catenas one can extrapolate ecosystem patterns for most of the biome.

Between the warm temperate to dry tropical savanna and the moist tropical miombo woodlands, mopane trees (*Colophospermum mopane*) form characteristic woodlands along the depressed, hot Limpopo, Shashi, Makgadikgadi and Okavango drainage systems. The leaves, shaped like a camel's foot, turn edge-on to the sun and provide little shade, so grass thrives even in the densest mopane forest where only cicadas and tsetse flies screech and buzz in the midday heat. Mopane leaves are highly nutritious and protein-rich so they are favoured by game, especially by elephants, and because they stay green long into the dry season the leaves can be browsed all year round. Cattle would like to get their teeth into the lush grasses of mopane woodlands, but tsetse flies - carriers of sleeping sickness - breed there and so the woodlands have to a great extent been left untouched as natural wildlife areas.

The biomass production of savanna grasslands is about 200

Left: *At night, the shrill and plaintive cry emitted from the trees around a camp-site is probably that of a galago or bushbaby. These fascinating, largely insectivor-ous creatures are excellent leapers and seldom descend to the ground.*
Above: *Warthogs often feed by crawling on their front knees for bulbs, tubers and grass rhizomes. Curiously, they are born with calluses on their knees, which may be the result of a convenient 'accident' of nature or of a need-related genetic re-sponse. Although natural selection seems to account for most of evolution's va-garies, the latest genetic research is slowly revealing a picture of 'active' and highly variable genes which can respond surprisingly quickly to environmental stimuli.*
Right: *This Sharpe's grysbok in Zimbabwe's Hwange National Park could easily be confused with the slightly larger steenbok.*

fruit off the ground. The Tonga people of southern Mozambique cel-ebrate their Feast of the First Fruit by pouring a marula concoction over the graves of their ancestors. Delicious preserves, jellies and al-coholic drinks are made from the fruit, while the seeds contain a pro-tein-rich oil that is used as a cosmetic and a soothing lotion. The seeds themselves are cooked or eaten raw and are used by sango-mas for divining. A potion made from the astringent bark is used to treat diarrhoea, and is thought to be a remedy for malaria.

The lack of strong relief throughout the Bushveld largely ac-counts for the feeling of unending, unchanging savanna, which is reinforced by the widespread distribution of many species. The biome's high species richness is a function of its enormous size rather than as a result of community diversity. The low rainfall and rich soils of the west seem to balance with the moist but dystrophic conditions of the east to increase the feeling of sameness that one ex-periences here. Although there are a number of endemic centres within the biome, the changes in community structure tend to be gradual, with a limited number of basic landscape-floristic patterns.

These 'toposequences' are called 'catenas' and they are used by ecologists in understanding the processes and states within such a large biome. Given information regarding the climate, soils and topography of an area, it is possible to predict the specific soil-vege-tation patterns that will exist in that catena. For instance, in a semi-arid environment fine-grained soils will creep down the hill slopes, leaving poor and stony soils above and richer, clay soils on the

times that of rain forests and the resulting herbivore biomass is un-equalled in any natural system, while the total biomass of all inver-tebrates here probably exceeds that of the herbivores. The second law of thermodynamics is central to all living systems and there is no better place to see it operating than in the food-chains of the Bush-veld. It is a complex law, but, put simply, it tells us that the universe tends towards a state of chaos. To create order we need to use en-ergy, which must be converted to some form of fuel and at every stage of conversion heat will be given off and radiate to the atmos-phere.

B·U·S·H·V·E·L·D B·I·R·D·S

At the top of the Bushveld food-chain are not lions, hyaenas or wild dogs, but vultures. They perform a vital role, that of sanitary inspectors and refuse disposers of the veld. Unfortunately they have been given a bad press by squeamish early European travellers and superstitious farmers alike, and have suffered mindless persecution as a result of it. Vultures are mostly thought of as ugly creatures, but to see them in flight is to see masters of the air, massive and graceful as they soar in the thermals hour after hour with scarcely a wingbeat. Although all vultures at

a carcass appear to be randomly tearing and squabbling, closer examination shows that fights are usually between members of the same species.

There are nine species of vulture in southern Africa, each with its own specialized niche. Those that live in the Bushveld have various levels of aggression and are equipped differently to spot carcasses and therefore arrive at different times. Their feeding requirements are similarly adapted to make use of different parts of a carcass. Some, such as the palm nut vulture (*Gypohierax angolensis*)

Left above: *Most visitors are attracted to the African bush to view large game and yet it is the fascinating birdlife that is more easily observed. The beautiful carmine bee-eater breeds in the eastern Caprivi, Chobe and Linyanti areas, as well as in northern Zimbabwe.*

Left below: *The booming territorial call of ground hornbills is initiated by one bird and then continued by another, as they inflate their stout throats, their scarlet wattles bulging.*

Above top: *The plumage of the lilac-breasted roller was used for the royal headdress of Chief Mzilikazi, founder of the Matabele nation.*

Above: *The exquisite white-fronted bee-eater roosts communally at night, but is mostly solitary during the day.*

Above right: *A white-backed vulture perches on an acacia tree, symbolizing its place at the top of the Kalahari's savanna food-pyramid.*

don't scavenge at all, but have become so specialized that they are in danger of becoming extinct as their palm-tree habitat disappears under man's onslaught. The Egyptian vulture (*Neophron percnopterus*) is even more endangered as a result of being subordinate to all other vultures at a kill. This is the 'law of the jungle' in operation.

Eagles of the Bushveld, like the African hawk eagle (*Hieraaetus fasciatus*), Wahlberg's eagle (*Aquila wahlbergi*) and bateleur (*Terathopius ecaudatus*) are themselves not averse to feeding from fresh carcasses as this expends far less energy than having to make a kill, and possibly failing. However, farmers are prone to leaving poisoned carcasses out for any 'vermin' that will take them. Eagle populations - and vultures, hyaenas and jackals as well - have in this way been severely reduced

in many areas of the Bushveld. Unfortunately, the law, in word, is on the side of the farmer who must protect his stock and therefore his livelihood. Regrettably, however, the farmers who practise unrestricted poisoning show little understanding of the veld on which they make a living. Some seem to care even less when shown by conservationists how best to co-exist with wild animals and to make positive use of them in management programmes.

Birds are the jewels of the Bushveld, ostentatiously decorating the trees and shrubs. Among the most vivid is the lilac-breasted roller (*Coracias caudata*) that gives flashing aerial displays while on the hunt for insects. Mzilikazi, founder of the Matebele nation, used the pastel-blue feathers of the roller for his royal headdress. Another is the crimson-

breasted shrike (*Laniarius atrococcineus*) which was named the 'Reichsvogel' by the German colonists of Namibia, as its brilliant red, white and black plumage reminded them of their national flag.

The smallest owl in southern Africa is the pearl-spotted owl (*Glaucidium perlatum*) which weighs only 7 grams at birth and 30 grams (the weight of a small tomato) when mature. However this diurnal hunter can kill lizards and bats of its own size. The white-faced owl (*Otus leucotis*) is an attractive, medium-sized, nocturnal owl that is often visible perching in a large tree during the day. The slightly smaller scops owl (*Otus senegalensis*) has similar habits but is usually overlooked during the day because of its excellent camouflage.

Seldom seen but well known by their melodious calling at dusk and on moonlit nights are the nightjars (*Caprimulgus* spp.), most spectacular of which is the partly diurnal pennant-winged nightjar, an intra-African migrant. During the breeding season the males give arresting flight displays to show off their streaming wing pennants, which are lost immediately after breeding.

Left: *A dark male ostrich accompanies two lighter-coloured females in the Kalahari Gemsbok National Park. Ostriches are found mainly in the arid western Bushveld and the desert regions and have been introduced into the Karoo. These large birds have lost many anatomical features required for flight, but they can run at speeds of up to 60 kilometres an hour and can defend themselves against predators with their powerful feet and legs.*

Above left: *The crested francolin keeps to dense savanna woodlands. Unlike its cousins of the fynbos and grassland areas, which are strong and willing fliers, this game bird seldom flies and escapes by running off into matted vegetation. It does, however, roost in trees.*

Above right: *The rufous-cheeked nightjar is an intra-African migrant. They lay their glossy pink to creamy-coloured eggs on the bare ground or on the leafy litter of plantations. Nightjars are particularly active in the twilight hours, when they swoop on flying insects with erratic beats of their wings.*

Right: *Spotted eagle owls are recognizable by their conspicuous ear-tufts. They are found in nearly every habitat in Southern Africa and they roost on the ground, in trees, on rocky ledges and even on city buildings.*

The basis of most food-chains is photosynthesis, whereby plants use about two per cent of available solar energy to produce new green material. This green material is eaten by herbivores such as antelope which, in turning plant matter to meat, retain about 10 per cent of absorbed plant energy; the rest is given off through respiration, urine and faeces, and reproductive processes. Carnivores in turn eat the herbivores and likewise convert a further 10 per cent of herbivore energy to body matter. In this way no energy is lost to the system, only to individual organisms.

All through the food-chain there are decomposers at work, busily returning nutrients to the system; vultures and hyaenas eat carcasses, dung beetles break down faeces, flies and bacteria invade any dead matter, consume it and convert it to body mass and excreta - nothing is wasted. But throughout this process organisms are jostling for a place in the hierarchy, competing for resources such as space, food and the opportunity to reproduce. The place that each organism occupies successfully is called its niche, and niches help to define the processes that drive the system.

White rhinos are grazers and so they manage to live side by side with black rhinos because the latter are browsers. However buffalo, white rhino, zebra, gazelles, some birds and termites are all grazers and would appear all to be competing for the same resources,

whereas they manage to live in the same habitat by finding distinct and separate niches there. They may be either nocturnal or diurnal, thus physically avoiding one another, but the majority of these animals live in a symbiotic relationship with one another.

A coarse stand of grass is not available to smaller animals with delicate mouths, and it may also conceal predators so they will avoid it until buffalo and elephants have trampled it down and eaten off the coarser top layer. Next zebras and wildebeest will move into that grass patch and eat the slightly less coarse material, with maybe a few new shoots. After these medium-sized herbivores have further refined the pasture and allowed for a considerable amount of re-shooting, the gazelles and hartebeest arrive to nip off the leafy parts and any juicy plants left by the larger animals. Next to arrive are birds such as Egyptian geese and doves which mow the short, new swards and pick up any fallen seeds. Finally, termites emerge to clear away the debris - and they provide food for the geese, bee-eaters, shrikes, aardwolfs, anteaters (aardvarks) and all other insectivores.

Once again nothing is wasted and all get enough to eat. But of course animals have evolved in response to the available resources and do not simply occupy a niche because it is there. On the other hand, because competition is so intense, if ever a niche becomes vacant or otherwise available, we can be sure that some species will

Below: *Buffalo love to graze in the rich glades of mopane woodlands. Often a lion will follow a herd of this size, preying only upon the weak, the young and the old, for a healthy, mature buffalo is a formidable foe.*
Right: *Baboons will eat almost anything and are especially adept at pulling the stings off the tails of scorpions, before popping the scorpions into their mouths. Highly sociable creatures, baboons will sometimes rally together at the approach of a leopard and the dominant males will attack first using their powerful jaws equipped with large canine teeth in a fearsome battle to the death.*

move in to occupy it, usually one with a catholic diet like elephants which graze and browse, eat fruit and seeds, roots and crops when they can.

Those who doubt that evolution is an active process, continually refining the physiologies and behaviour of organisms to best utilize their environments, need only consider the wide but subtle range of gazelle-like antelope that inhabit southern Africa. First there are the dainty springbok that inhabit the western grasslands and desert; they are mainly grazers but browse small bushes and can survive without drinking. Next, the impala's distribution fits the springbok's like a jigsaw puzzle piece, being confined to the mois-

ter savanna woodlands; it is mainly a browser but also grazes and cannot survive without drinking regularly.

Lechwe are confined to the floodplains of the Okavango-Caprivi area; they graze or eat aquatic plants, preferring to feed in the shallow water of flood plains. Puku are found only in the extreme eastern tip of the Caprivi and Chobe area; they graze in open grasslands adjoining swamps. Finally, the waterbuck are grazers that may be found on stony ground some way away from water. The same niche-related adaptions are to be found in antelope such as kudu, nyala, bushbuck and sitatunga as well as in zebra and elephant - to name but the more obvious examples.

But while herbivores are often to be seen milling around the same waterhole or pasture, competition at the top of the food-chain is too intense to allow for close species interaction. Studies have shown that lions, cheetahs and even leopards have a fairly low hunting success rate. Cheetahs kill with speed on the open plains but they are frail compared with lions or hyaenas and have to eat quickly to avoid having their meals stolen by these more robust carnivores. Leopards avoid this competition to some extent by taking small prey in dense woodlands and then dragging it into high thorn trees where they can eat at leisure. Hyaenas, contrary to the belief of many, are good hunters and are often more successful than lions. They also do not hesitate to steal prey away from other carnivores, including lions, and to scavenge. In fact what tourists see as hyaenas 'scavenging' off lion kills by day is more likely to be the final episode of a nocturnal hunt where a hyaena kill has been stolen by lions and the hyaenas have returned to claim their meagre share.

Lions are the only wild cats to form prides, which can number up to 30 individuals. They are large, powerful carnivores, weighing up to 230 kilograms, but they seem averse to physical exertion, moving swiftly only when hunting or aroused to anger. They have no natural enemies and can take their pick from any prey animal, including the fearsome buffalo. They breed throughout the year. One would expect them to have enormous potential for reducing herbivore populations but actually the balance between carnivores and herbivores is dictated by the number of herbivores. While herbivores may abound on the plains, there is only as much food as a carnivore can catch and if the herbivores migrate, carnivore numbers will drop off with a lag effect. While pride members will often co-operate in a kill, eating is strictly on a strongest-eat-first basis. If there is not enough to go round, cubs may die and young adults will have to leave the pride to survive. The 'king of beasts' may seem a lazy, near-obsolete element in the fiercely competitive savanna ecosystem, yet his awesome size and disdainful dignity makes him the most compelling creature of the African wilds.

Whereas essentially solitary hyaenas are opportunists, wild dogs are the most remarkable social carnivores, their very survival depending on total co-operation in hunting. A hunting dog is no bigger than a jackal and left to themselves they would either starve or be killed by the larger predators. But a pack of wild dogs can run down a wildebeest or zebra, and unlike the larger carnivores they seldom fail in a hunt. These dogs work as a team, selecting an animal and then separating it from its herd, harassing and confusing it until they have run it down. The dogs work in relays so as not to tire themselves out and so their victim gets no respite.

While lion prides fluctuate and change members as needs dictate, a pack of wild dogs is a permanent clan that becomes more and more efficient with time, thereby also reducing aggression between members. Visitors to game reserves seldom see the lethal efficiency of a wild dog kill, but if they do they will usually comment on how

'inhumane' it is, for the dogs will begin to rip at the prey's soft underbelly and eat while the animal is still gasping for breath. Few of these people consider the unusual orderliness with which the dogs go about their meal; each takes its fill according to a strict hierarchy and if there isn't enough to go round the first time, the pack will hunt again and again until every hunter, mother and pup has had its fill.

Man is the super predator, his superior brain being the reason for his dominance for he can remember the past, reflect on the present and act for the future. It was here in the African savanna that he was born some four million years ago and for most of his time on earth he was a nomadic hunter-gatherer much like the Kalahari Bushmen of today. But a few thousand years ago mankind's reasoning abilities took great leaps forward, and he learned how to cultivate wild cereals and to domesticate herd animals. And so his resource requirements changed to meet his new lifestyle. He depended on a constant supply of water and grazing, still essentially nomadic but staying for longer and longer periods to plant and harvest crops. Social groups expanded around these newly available food sources and so villages, then towns and eventually whole empires came into existence. But the Bushveld has a predictable drought cycle, and to survive this humans still had to follow the water and grazing.

Then to Africa came European colonists who created political

Left: *Burchell's or plains zebra are highly dependent on water and grazing and will travel great distances in search of both requirements. Seen here in the Savuti region of the Chobe National Park, large herds are also still found widely over northern Namibia.*

Above: *The hunter and explorer, Captain Cornwallis Harris, is the first white man known to have seen the attractive sable antelope. It is a grazer which avoids both dense woodlands and short grasslands, preferring to be near permanent water in the tall grass of open woodlands; unfortunately bush encroachment and overgrazing have degraded much of its former habitat. The bulls are aggressive fighters and will ably defend themselves against lions, leopards and wild dogs, using their rapier-sharp horns.*

Right: *Experts at concealment, kudu prefer the densest bush. They are mainly browsers and their wide choice of food and taste for crops has allowed them to survive where the sable has been displaced.*

Previous spread: *The blue wildebeest is often referred to as the 'clown' of the Bushveld. Certainly, they are curious, ungainly bovids, but their numbers suggest that they are among the most successful large animals in Africa. Wildebeest are close relatives of the hartebeest, bontebok, blesbok and tsessebe, all of the subfamily Alcelaphinae.*

Left: *Most elephant charges are mock attacks, but are terrifying all the same. Elephants should be approached with the greatest of caution and avoided if one is on foot. Cows are particularly nervous when accompanied by their young and will not hesitate to attack. It is foolish to be lulled into a false sense of security by stories about poor eyesight - in spite of this these huge animals are agile and fast and can charge without warning.*

Above: *Serval are fairly common in the moist southern, eastern and northern parts of the sub-continent. Once hunted mercilessly, these inoffensive cats are now protected in some parts of their range.*

Above right: *In the bush one learns not to be too familiar with lions, leopards and elephants, and honey badgers should be added to this list. Although shy and elusive, they are utterly fearless and tough animals. Even lions are unlikely to escape lightly from a tussle with a honey badger.*

---

boundaries where none had previously existed; they brought with them medicines and technology that allowed populations to swell and towns and cities erupted on the face of the continent. The colonists also imposed laws and regulations that fettered the traditional lifestyles of the people. And so now people were forced to live on marginal lands, and when the inevitable droughts came, there they had to stay. To practise their pastoral lifestyle, traditional people use two techniques to drive nature back: they slash the woodlands back for fuel and to increase the grazing lands, and they burn the grasslands to stimulate new growth.

Many plants here have fire resistant bark, such as *Protea caffra*, the Transvaal boekenhout (*Faurea saligna*) and baobabs which can survive the most severe fires and even flourish when their trunks have been hollowed out. Usually there is less than 10 per cent die-off after Bushveld fires, when plants that have experienced 'top kill'

resprout from their bases or rebud below ground. In many instances the below-ground age of plants may be many times greater than the above-ground growth. Geophytes (plants growing from bulbs or similar underground structures) and grasses burst with new shoots soon after bush fires and this quickly attracts grazers.

The savanna is a fire-evolved ecosystem and without periodic burning many of its plants would become moribund and die off. But too frequent burning does it immeasurable harm. Trees are burned too soon to seed, the veld is denuded too often and erosion begins, important nitrogen-producing micro-organisms in the soil are destroyed and so the environment becomes locked into a cycle of degradation.

Bushmen are probably our closest link with primeval Africa. They live in simple harmony with their surroundings, and their numbers are too small to have widespread effects on the environment. In traditional settings, Bushmen have no private property, no permanent homes and few possessions. This lifestyle is in fact a function of the transient resources of their world and necessary for their survival. Once they populated much of South Africa but their gentle ways were no match for the more aggressive black tribes and certainly not for the firearms of the invading whites. Rapidly they were pushed further and further westwards until only a few remained in the Kalahari and Namibia. Sadly, there are no longer any Bushmen living in a natural state, even in the Kalahari, for a decade of drought forced the last bands to congregate around state-supplied boreholes or around army camps where their amazing tracking skills are utilized in the Namibian bush war. The police also use them to track thieves and other miscreants. But here their delicate social codes break down and they begin to lose that unique relationship with nature, turning to the vices that plague all people who have become displaced by the modern technological world.

Summer in the Bushveld lasts for between six and eight blazing months. The heat is temporarily relieved by thunderstorms that usually fall from November through to February. After a decade of consistently good rains the herds are fat and have reproduced copiously. The carnivores too have been fattened by killing off the weaker herbivores, the trees support heavy canopies of leaves and the grass sways golden in the summer breezes. But it is a deceptive richness that tricks animals into over-indulgence, for next will come a decade of drought and relentless heat that will suck up all the water and scorch the grass. Then the large herbivores will move off to find new pastures and water. Many will die along the way, and the predators which have grown lazy will soon be fighting over territories as food supplies diminish.

This happened during the extreme drought that spanned the 1970s and 1980s, when carcasses littered the veld from from one side of the continent to the other.

The effects of drought and overstocking are most severely felt in reserves with limited land, where fences prevent game from migrating when conditions impel them to move on. Many die along the fence lines, their sinews sliced and bones snapped by the taut wires, dry hides left to flap in the burning winds like tattered plastic bags. For some time there has been talk of private game reserves in the Lowveld taking down all their adjoining fences, and thereby giving the Kruger National Park managers the incentive to follow their example. This would greatly expand the range of Lowveld animals and lead to far more efficient ecosystem management.

But not all Lowveld landowners have such progressive ideas about resource management. The system of land tenure in South Africa and the tradition of exploitation has made many farmers jealous of the land they control and eager to exploit any game that steps on it. Some farmers are known to lure game out of the reserves and into the sights of ruthless trophy-hunters' rifles. Even the celebrated white lions of the Timbavati reserve were subjected to this treatment. The same is true of water resources, where private landowners restrict the river flow even into reserves like the Kruger National Park and Kalahari Gemsbok National Park so that they can exploit the land for short-term financial gain.

An impressive resource management programme has been implemented in parts of Zimbabwe, where game reserves have taken down fences and allowed the game to move out into the surrounding rural trust lands. At the same time the local farmers have voluntarily congregated in central villages where, with state subsidies, they build new homes and kraals. Communal, rotating grazing lands are fenced off and controlled according to advice from agricultural extension officers, which leaves the surrounding Bushveld clear to regenerate and absorb the game.

Each community decides how it will manage its new resource opportunities, and so some choose to utilize the game for meat, taking advantage of the greater conversion rate of plant matter to protein afforded by game. Others have chosen to run cattle and wild species, such as eland, impala, sable and kudu which can graze and browse and are resistant to many of the plants that cattle find unpalatable or toxic, on the same land. Another option is to use the reclaimed wilderness as hunting grounds and gain revenue by selling hunting licences. Because trophy hunters are not interested in meat and hides, these resources may be used or sold according to the wishes of the village headman.

In the schemes already operating, communities that not long ago were facing ruin and starvation have now managed to feed themselves, have had boreholes sunk and have built schools from cash brought in. When a problem animal threatens a community, rangers from the nearest reserve are called in to shoot the animal. If it is an elephant, for instance, the meat is shared by the community while the hide and tusks are sold to compensate for any damage and to swell their coffers. If crops are destroyed, the victim receives a state allotment of grain. In this way rural communities are able to benefit directly from conservation management and poaching is all but eliminated.

Equally important is that the natural gene pool is able to expand its range and its interactive potential, and a balance is recreated between man and his natural environment. Only through far-sighted resource management schemes such as this will the Bushveld be able to retain its internal integrity and survive for our children to grow up having all the benefits of modern technology, but tempered by a knowledge of untamed Africa and all its wonders.

Left: *To witness a cheetah charging its prey is a thrilling experience. This cheetah was seen at the start of its awesome sprint in the Kruger National Park.*
Right above: *An nyala bull is perhaps even more striking than its closest relative, the kudu. Nyalas occur in the dense bush and riverine forests of the game reserves of Zululand, in the Kruger National Park and in south-eastern Zimbabwe and neighbouring Mozambique.*
Right below: *Most of Africa's dung beetles belong to the very large family Scarabidae, or scarab beetles as they are more commonly known. Their dung balls play an important role throughout the beetles' life cycles. They eat the dung, and with the food balls males attract females to their underground chambers to mate. The eggs are laid in a new dung ball, wherein the larvae hatch and soon begin eating. When the dung has been consumed, the larvae pupate inside the dung-encrusted hole. When the adults emerge, the cycle begins again.*

Grasslands

AS THE FIRST BLADES OF LIGHT CUT the crisp winter air on the Highveld, tiny ice droplets glow on the grass seed-heads, like miniature crystal earrings. The sunlight grows stronger and animals begin to stir, the frost melts and drips onto the ground, where fine root-hairs wait just below the surface to suck up the moisture. If at this time you put your ear to the ground, as do bat-eared foxes, you might discern a faint scratching sound coming from within.... In termite nests below the ground termite nymphs that have been fed special food begin to grow wing stumps in mysterious anticipation of spring.

From September the morning frosts become lighter and the days steadily warmer. In October the sky invites fluffy white cumulus clouds to frolic in the warm afternoon air; now the termite nymphs have grown wings and they start to develop a hard, black skin in preparation for their first and only excursion beyond their underground world. The grass is still dry and brittle, and, like the termites, eager for the promise of rain.

Now the afternoon clouds swell and bruise with heavy water droplets. By late October the cumulo-nimbus clouds are leaping high in the rising thermals - eight, nine thousand metres above the ground. The afternoons are charged with anticipation, for if the rains do not come soon the land will wither in the heat and lightning will ignite the tinder-dry grass. Then one day, probably in early November, the sky turns black, lightning and thunder begin their daily bombardments and a bracing wind crackles through the dry veld. A fat drop of water lands on the startled ground, and then another, and another and within seconds the churning clouds let loose a torrent of rain that freshens the fatigued land.

Powerful thermal engines within the churning clouds circulate the drops of water and with each cycle the drops grow bigger and colder, freezing in the high atmosphere until the balls of ice become too heavy to hold, and soon hail stones are beating on the muddy ground and stripping leaves from branches and punching blooms from their stems. Then, as suddenly as it started, so the rain and hail cease, the clouds dissipate and sunlight slaps a rainbow across a rain-fresh sky. Water trickles down past the termite nests where the nymphs have by now become fully developed males and females, ready to make their nuptial flights that will enable them to form breeding couples and begin new colonies.

This storm is also a signal for the bat-eared foxes, the lizards, birds, antbears, hedgehogs and even wild cats to emerge from their shelters, for they know that soon begins an annual feast. Wingless worker termites which for weeks have been busily digging tunnels to the surface finally break through the damp ground and out pour millions upon millions of winged termites, filling the air in whirling masses. But their flight is weak and clumsy and soon they return to earth, drop their wings and rush about to locate a mate. Then they must begin tunnelling to avoid being eaten by the creatures that are gobbling up this shower of nutrients.

Left: *The kori bustard is a massive bird of the more arid grasslands, where it eats just about everything, including insects, rodents, seeds and carrion. Its taste for acacia gum gives this heaviest of all flying birds the Afrikaans name of* gompou.

Termite mounds are the punctuation marks on the African plains, and can be thought of as city states under strict authoritarian control, where sterile workers and soldiers toil day and night in total obedience, without the distractions of sex. Termitaria house populations comparable to the largest human cities, and they are made possible by a complex social system that is by far the oldest on earth. South Africa's most creative naturalist, Eugéne Marais, likened termitaria to living organisms. He studied them over many years and

Left: *Blue wildebeest have been re-introduced to their grassland habitat in the Rustenburg Nature Reserve. This area, demarcated by the Magaliesberg range, is an ecotone between the grassland and bushveld ecosystems.*
Above: *The timid aardwolf is a nocturnal, insectivorous animal which eats mainly termites. Despite this, it is persecuted by farmers because of its resemblance to hyaenas and jackals.*
Right: *Termites are possibly the most important grazers of the grasslands. Their termitaria are highly complex structures, which have been likened to living organisms, each complete with a durable, elastic skin, as well as circulatory, digestive and central nervous systems. From her eternally dark royal chamber, the immobile, grub-like queen directs all the activities of the colony - but no-one has yet discovered how this is done.*

perceived each colony to have an elastic skin that is self-healing, a circulation system, digestive system and even a central nervous system and a communications network.

It is not known how signals are transmitted through the colony, especially since colonies are difficult to study under natural conditions. Marais was fortunate to find a termite nest without an outside skin under the floorboards of an old house near Pretoria, which gave him access to even the secret royal chamber. By candle-

light he observed the plump queen, surrounded by a Praetorian guard of soldiers; he saw them arranging themselves in patterns around the queen and each time she moved, it seemed as if a message was being conveyed throughout the colony to perform a specific duty.

The mounds are constructed with a cement made from soil and the insects' pasty excrement; they are are weather-proof, air-conditioned, durable structures, strong enough to keep out their many enemies. Termites (sometimes wrongly called white ants) are delicate, blind creatures living in a perpetually moist, dark environment, and if a mound is breached they are easy prey for ants, their most bitter foes. When this happens soldiers and workers rush to the opening and throw themselves into guarding and repair work as a matter of life and death. As the population of the colony expands the mound is enlarged, thus solving the sewage problems of these vast underground cities.

In arid grasslands termites and then locusts are the most important grazers, consuming more grass than all the mammalian herbivores. They process plant material and turn it into a more concentrated form of energy, and in doing so they become the second level of food available in the system. But they are also the most important real-estate developers there, for when a termitarium is vacated there is a host of other creatures - other insects, geckos and snakes - that are ready to move in.

It is not unusual to find a large rinkhals (*Hemachatus haemachatus*) sharing an old termite mound with geckos and shrews alike. The rinkhals is confined to the South African grasslands, with a small relict population found at Inyanga in the eastern highlands of Zimbabwe. These poisonous snakes are often found close to human habitation, in garden rockeries and compost heaps. They are spitting cobras whose accurate jet of venom can blind an intruder. If a rinkhals is molested it is likely to sham death, going limp but keeping a wary eye on opportunities for escape. Anyone fooled into touching the snake will receive an injection of potentially lethal neurotoxin, typical of the family Elapidae snakes (cobras, mambas and coral snakes).

Another real-estate developer of the grasslands is the noctur-

nal aardvark (*Orycteropus afer*) which excavates holes in even the hardest ground for shelter or to gain access to its food, using a long, slime-coated tongue to probe ant and termite nests. Many animals including hyaenas, reptiles, insects, small mammals and numerous bird species depend on their excavations for shelter. But aardvark holes in roads, airstrips, farmlands and earth dams are a danger, often causing broken axles and burst dams. If directly threatened, aardvarks will begin burrowing and they can outdig any pursuer; a Victorian naturalist reported that a team of people using spades and picks for eight hours gave up the chase after digging a tunnel 32 metres long. During the rainy season antbear burrows are often flooded, and, as the animals lie asleep on dry ground during the day, they fall easy prey to predators, human or otherwise.

In moist grasslands earthworms are tireless excavators, helping to turn over soil and to aerate it, thereby speeding up the development of organic-rich topsoil and improving soil drainage. The worms consume organic detritus and excrete nutrients directly into the soil, carrying leaf litter underground where bacteria also help to break it down. Like termites, earthworms perform important biological functions within the ground and they also make juicy meals for hadedas and hedgehogs.

At night, when owls go silently hunting, the inoffensive little hedgehogs (*Atelerix frontalis*) go foraging for worms, insects and fungi. While even lions seem unable to harm hedgehogs when curled in their defensive spiky balls, their defences are no protection against the long talons and sharp beak of the giant eagle owl (*Bubo lacteus*). Eagle owl roosts can often be located in large trees by the piles of discarded hedgehog skins below them.

Grassland ecosystems occur throughout the central plateau region of South Africa, and also in parts of the Savanna and Karoo-Nama biomes, where they reach into the Natal and Transkei midlands and montane areas up to an altitude of about 2 850 m, through much of the eastern and central Cape, with isolated semi-aquatic outliers occuring around the swamps and pans of Etosha, Makgadikgadi, the Okavango/Linyanti area and the Ovamboland *dambos*. These *dambo* swamps occur where poor drainage causes the ground to become waterlogged in the rainy season, but then it completely dries out through the dry season. Only grasses can survive such extremes. *Hyphaene* palms and underground forest species may be found growing on higher ground at the limits of seasonal waterlogging.

Grass is the most successful form of life on earth, because most of its growing effort goes into reproduction, making copious seedheads which are supported by a thin stem with sparse leaves. When conditions are right they are able to flourish and reproduce quickly through seeding or coppicing. The plants have deep roots to take advantage of penetrating rains, as well as tiny surface root-hairs that can absorb the finest moisture in the topsoil. Grass can grow under the most extreme conditions: in the polar regions, in the most arid deserts or on volcanic rock. Once grass has established itself in a new habitat, it begins to modify the biotic environment by breaking down rock to form soil, enriching that soil with its own dead litter.

In southern Africa by far the most important and widespread grass is *Themeda triandra*, more commonly known as rooigras. In most grasslands it is a climax species, but overgrazing over many centuries has severely reduced its abundance in all but the sour montane habitats where it forms a distinct community with *Festuca costata* tussock grass. Overgrazing is one of the most serious problems that threatens our natural ecosystems, and is itself a function of overpopulation.

Research has shown, however, that in Transkei, where the sour pastures have over the past 30 years been overstocked by two to four

times the accepted First World standard, the veld there still has a high proportion of climax grass species and a high percentage of cover. This raises many doubts about currently held ideas concerning optimal stocking rates. It seems that where overstocking is extreme the goats, cattle and sheep eat all the veld grasses and not just the tastier ones, as they do in selective overgrazing. Then when the veld does revive, all species re-emerge in the same proportions as before, not giving the unfavoured species a chance to dominate.

From the diaries and paintings of early travellers through the interior we are told of endless vistas of golden grasslands where vast game herds grazed the sweet shoulder-high grasses. It is legend that some of these herds of migrating springbok and black wildebeest took two or three days to pass stationary wagons. Animals such as the quagga (*Equus quagga*) were also so numerous that hunters and Voortrekkers simply shot every one that came into their sights until there were none left. Today most of this area is covered by semi-desert scrub and maize. Farmers who settled on the central pastures could not tolerate predators and so lions and cheetah were soon exterminated. Apparently a favourite sport was to chase cheetahs across the open plains on horseback and as they tired, to club them down with stirrup irons.

An animal endemic to the sweet grasslands which has, fortunately, survived, despite being heavily hunted for meat and hides, is the blesbok (*Damaliscus dorcas phillipsi*). It is a subspecies of the bontebok (*D. dorcas dorcas*), both forms having distinctive white facial markings, but the bontebok has more white on its rump, belly and flanks. The bontebok is found only within the Fynbos Biome and blesbok were only recorded after early explorers had traversed the scrub Karoo and reached the Eastern Cape grasslands. Although both subspecies were shot nearly to extinction, they have been reintroduced to reserves and farms. The blesbok is, along with the springbok, one of South Africa's most important farm-game species.

The problem of the sweetveld was that while it offered excellent grazing, it was found in the drier south-western areas of the central Cape where the soils are less leached and more nutritious but which is not suited to intensive stocking. Wild herds would migrate to and from the sweetveld to take advantage of good rains, and then move off when the food became depleted, giving it time to recover. It only took a few seasons of domestic herds, selectively overgrazing the tastier grasses, to allow unpalatable thorn bushes and scrub from the drier western Karoo to begin invading the sweetveld. The next step of desertification is that without grass cover, wind and water from flash floods allow the thin layer of topsoil to be stripped away, imperceptibly at first perhaps, but inexorably.

J.P.H. Acocks was a tireless ecologist, employed by the South African Department of Agriculture to study the effects of agriculture on the land. For about 20 years he travelled the byways of the country, mapping all the veld types and observing the spread of desert and semi-desert flora from the dry west into other ecosystems as a result of man's presence there over the past 600 years. His volume entitled 'Veld Types of South Africa' is probably the most often quoted scientific text in southern Africa and one of the sub-conti-

Left: *Biogeography considers the relationships between species and their environments, and how the different species relate to each other genetically. 'Corridors', such as rivers or island archipelagos, may assist the spread of certain species, while 'barriers', such as deserts, mountains and oceans, may impede them. As continents shift, species may be separated or allowed to mix, and changing climates may also divide or join species. In southern Africa, there are several populations of helmeted guinea-fowl, separated geographically and distinguishable by their slightly different head casques.*

nent's most important ecological works. Acocks worked out that sweet grasses had once covered nearly all of the South African interior; by following demographic and climatic trends, he calculated that by the year 2050 desert and semi-desert karoid vegetation would cover virtually all of the the Cape Province beyond the Fynbos Biome, the Orange Free State, all of Lesotho, and a large portion of the south-western Transvaal. The economically important sweetveld would then be reduced to a small island in the Standerton/Bethal area.

Typical sweet grasses are the fine *Panicum* and *Eragrostis* species (panic and lovegrasses respectively) with their delicate flower-heads that are common among the alien cosmos along roadsides and in other disturbed areas. Through overgrazing they have been largely replaced in the open veld by sour species such as the giant turpentine grass (*Cymbopogon validus*), Ngongoni bristlegrass (*Aristida junciformis*) and the dark green tussock grass, *Festuca costata*.

The Grassland Biome itself is a summer rainfall area, with extensive hailfalls and winter frost, which in places can occur up to 180 days a year. Rainfall is generally higher than in the Savanna Biome, and the moisture regime benefits by having a much lower evapo-transpiration rate than in the savanna. With the exception of the pan areas, these grasslands are undulating plains, draining into the Vaal, Caledon and Orange rivers to the west and the Crocodile, Phongola, Thukela, Umzimvubu and the Kei rivers to the east.

The grassland vegetation follows a three-dimensional gradient, the axes of which are altitude, latitude - both of which determine temperature - and moisture. When there is a suitable overlap between these three factors, grasslands are likely to be found. It is believed that most grasslands are maintained through poor drainage, through centuries of stock grazing and burning to promote grazing, and by the occurrence of frost - all of which give trees little chance to establish themselves.

Common wisdom tells us that when the Voortrekkers arrived on the Highveld they found a grassland paradise little changed from

Previous spread: *The sweet-grass plains which encircle the Etosha, Makgadikgadi and other pans of the arid west support large herds of grazers. Zebra eat the coarser, longer grasses, and springbok eat the softer shoots and leaves.*
Left: *Much of the common knowledge we have about animal behaviour originates from early hunters and explorers, whose observations are not always borne out by contemporary research. It was held, for instance, that the nocturnal spring-hare emerges from its burrow with a high leap, but records tell of a more circumspect exit, with the twitching nose emerging cautiously to test the air.*
Above: *Under natural conditions blesbok were confined to the grasslands. They have been widely introduced to the Karoo and the south-eastern Kalahari, and have survived wherever there are sweet grazing lands and permanent water.*

the time of Creation. In fact, what they unknowingly witnessed was the final episode of a saga that had brought untold suffering to the people of southern Africa. The white pioneers moved into a depopulated land that only 20 years previously had been a more or less peaceful, prosperous land of Iron-age pastoralists.

From about the 1400s, black tribes had been moving into and settling in the central and eastern grasslands of southern Africa and it is this human presence that had for the most part created the grassland ecosystems. They herded cattle and planted sorghum, and mined the hillsides for iron, copper and gold ores from which they forged empires such as that to be seen in the great ruins of Zimbabwe. These people regularly burned the veld to bring new shoots for their herds to graze, and this practice is thought to have kept the trees at bay.

However, some ecologists now believe that it was the need for charcoal to process the metal ores that were used for weapons, tools and ornaments that now accounts for the almost total lack of trees found in the Grassland Biome. In the same way the once plentiful

forests of northern Africa and the Middle East fuelled the Roman Empire; with the help of a changing climate this over-exploitation reduced those areas to deserts. History is repeating itself before our eyes: so is much of southern Africa being reduced from forest to grassland, and then in places from grassland to wasteland.

In the early 19th-century, growing populations and the competition for limited grazing and crop lands, compounded by the arrival of land-hungry white settlers, led to the emergence of powerful warlords among the black tribes. For a decade they waged war across much of southern Africa, laying it waste. The greatest of these was Shaka, who welded the tribes of northern Natal into the fierce Zulu nation, but there were others like Matiwane and Mzilikazi, both emanating from Shaka's domain, and the amazonian Mantatisi of the Cat People who had a fearful reputation as the exterminator of Sotho-speaking tribes. Perhaps the most intriguing of these leaders was Moshesh, who brought together all the stragglers of these *Difaqane* wars and withdrew with them into the mountainous central plateau to form the Basotho nation.

The *Difaqane* wars lasted from about 1820 to the end of that decade and were followed by ten years of drought. Some of the people left in this area were living in the sheltered forests, many had joined the larger tribes beyond the battlegrounds, while others in desperation had turned to cannibalism to survive and were living in caves along the foothills of the Drakensberg and Malutis.

Without modern technology to alter the state of basic resources, it is interesting to observe how the large and small forms in an ecosystem resemble one another, by being locked into the same energy cycle and having the same resources to hand. An example of this may be the huts of indigenous grassland pastoralists who built their homes out of grass and mud, and who made their floors from a mixture of clay and cow dung - similar materials to those used by termites to build their mounds.

But the white settlers brought with them new technology and a social structure unlike anything that was known in Africa. They had sophisticated means of harnessing power and could pump water to their fields, build strong forts and houses, cure diseases and

Left: *Steenbok are associated with open grasslands, including airstrips, firebreaks and cultivated lands.*
Above: *Most people think that the name of the secretary-bird refers to the quill-like tuft of feathers on the back of its head. In fact, it is a corruption of its Arabic name, meaning hunting bird.*
Below: *The elegant grasshopper* Zonocerus elegans, *found throughout most of sub-saharan Africa, exudes a foul-smelling fluid as a defence mechanism.*

obtain higher food yields from the land. Destitute black people flocked to their farms with the promise of food, shelter and protection from the ravages they had known. With superior technology and cheap and plentiful labour, the open veld was steadily transformed into maize-fields and fenced range-lands. When diamonds and then gold were discovered in the interior a tide of urbanization began to flow across the grasslands, a tide that threatens to be as prodigious as the oceans.

Few wild animals could withstand such widespread intrusions into their habitat, especially not the large herbivores that were now forced to compete with domestic herds for grazing and the large predators that hunted them but which found small stock easier meat. Smaller cats such as caracal are still found on the High-veld where they hunt birds, dassies, rodents and livestock. If their predilection for sheep and goats alone did little to enhance their status among farmers, caracal also have a reputation for going on 'killing frenzies', getting into sheep kraals where they may kill up to 20 animals in a night. Small mammals such as mongooses and hares are still plentiful, but it is the birds that have best managed to cope with the intrusions of man and even to integrate their lifestyles with that of human habitation.

Francolin and helmeted guinea-fowl are common and visible residents of the grasslands, as are the long-legged species like crowned plovers, korhaans and the massive Stanley's and kori bustards. Even more common but seldom noticed are the cisticolas. These small, dull-brown warblers are very common in all grasslands, where they hang on grass stems, tails often fanned out and flicking.

A bird which fares well in cultivated lands, by eating seeds from standing crops, is the blue crane (*Anthropoides paradisea*). Farmers often lay down poisoned seed in their fields to kill it, and only the fact that it is South Africa's national bird saves it from wider persecution. They are tall, attractive birds that entertained the Voortrekkers with their mating dances, as the pioneers' wagons dragged slowly across the undulating veld.

At least one animal thrives on the destruction of the grasslands, and that is the spring-hare (*Pedetes capensis*). It is a nocturnal rodent that lives where sandy soils allow it to burrow, such as are found around Lake Ngami and the Makgadikgadi Salt Pans in Botswana. Spring-hares survive here by nipping off the seed-heads and green buds from the closely cropped grass, as it tries to recover from heavy overgrazing. The cattle farmers of these areas still cling to their pastoral way of life, despite relying more heavily on spring-hares for food than on their domestic herds.

Fynbos Region

IN MANY WAYS the south-western tip of Africa is a world apart, isolated in sense and form from the rest of the sub-continent of southern Africa; in appearance it is like an old and craggy face which every season receives the attention of the nature's finest make-up artist to compensate for its old age, its poor diet and its cracked and flaking skin. The climatic extremes and the contorted landscape create the complex natural environment which harbours by far the smallest and yet richest of the world's six floral kingdoms.

The Cape Floral Kingdom extends roughly from Vanrhynsdorp in the north-west to Humansdorp in the east. This is the area of the Cape Supergroup of rocks that were laid down as marine and deltaic sediments between 500 and 350 million years ago - a period that spans most of the Palaeozoic era (Ordovician, Silurian and Devonian periods). They rest on top of older Cape Granites and Malmesbury Group shales which can be clearly seen in the Peninsula area, forming the gentler slopes below the sandstone cliffs of the mountains. Cruise along Chapman's Peak Drive and you will notice how the shale and sandstone cliffs lie directly on paler, more rounded granite rocks that tumble steeply down to the sea.

The first group of rocks of the Cape system is the Table Mountain Group, composed mainly of coarse quartzitic sandstones alternating with thin bands of shale that were laid down in shallow marine waters of the Agulhas Basin; these rocks are generally referred to as Table Mountain Sandstone (TMS). After this period inland conditions must have changed, for over the next period the deposits in the basin were not marine sands but were brought down by eight main delta systems flowing from the northern highlands and Gondwanaland's Atlantic Mountains to the west. They deposited mostly shale sediments, with thin sandstone layers in between, on top of the TMS to form the Bokkeveld Group of rocks. After this period conditions similar to that of the TMS period resumed and the Witteberg sediments were deposited on top of the Bokkeveld, resembling the TMS but generally softer and more easily eroded.

The TMS group of rocks is the oldest of the Cape Supergroup that was laid down in horizontal layers, and therefore generally lies at the bottom of the group. Through folding, however, and subsequent erosion, the upper layers of soft Bokkeveld shales and Witteberg sandstones have been whittled away from the upward-thrust folds to leave the bases of TMS as reminders of mountains that once stood 6 000 metres high. The Bokkeveld shales now form the long valleys between the parallel ranges of folded mountains, with Witteberg sandstones being confined to ridges along the northern margin of the system. The shales weather to form clayey soils that are far richer than those derived from sandstones and so the valleys are fertile and highly prized for agriculture.

Left: *The mountain zebra has two distinct subspecies: Hartmann's mountain zebra is found in the mountains of the Namibian escarpment and Kaokoveld, and the Cape mountain zebra shown here lives in the fynbos or grassland of the Cape Fold mountains. Both subspecies are well adapted to harsh, dry conditions and have a dewlap below the throat.*

Valleys such as the Hex River, Franschhoek, Het Land van Waveren around Tulbagh and Wolseley, and others, surrounded by the Groot Drakenstein, Kleinwinterhoek, and Witzenberg mountains, and the mighty Hex River Mountains themselves, are famous for their wine and fruit, their graceful Cape Dutch farmhouses and picturesque historical towns. But farming in these fertile valleys and on the coastal plains has meant that the relatively luxuriant shrublands that grew on the richer soils there have been reduced to less than 10 per cent of their former extent. It is only in the harsh mountain areas with their poor soils and climatic extremes that the Cape's flora survives to an acceptable degree - but even here it is threatened by an invasion of of another kind.

Early foresters in the Cape were faced with three main tasks: to establish fast-growing timber plantations to replace the denuded natural forests of the area, to stabilize the wide tracts of shifting sands of the Cape Flats and along the coast, and to grow trees on what they considered to be barren mountain slopes. The first objective was quite easily achieved by planting exotic pines and gum trees. The umbrella-topped stone pine (*Pinus pinea*) posed few immediate problems, but species like the cluster pine (*P. pinaster*), being self-seeding, spread into the surrounding mountains where they now pose a great threat to the fynbos.

To stabilize the dunes was a task that took much longer to accomplish, but after experimenting with many plants from other Mediterranean areas, Australian acacias proved just the thing. Today rooikrans and Port Jackson willow (*Acacia cyclops* and *A. saligna*)

have spread rapidly through the fynbos and indeed frequent veld fires have aided their infestation of the natural flora. The third objective was met by giving seeds from Australian hakeas and pines to mountaineers to sow as they walked. It took time for the plan to reach fruition, but today hakeas and pines are so well established in the folded mountains that the state spends vast sums in attempts to control these alien invaders.

'Hacking' the hakea is a favourite pastime among conservationists and a regular job for forestry workers, but this barely stems the tide of invasion. The final answer to the invasion problem is to be found in biological controls, with the introduction of natural predators from the invasive plants' countries of origin. The problem with introducing the organisms into the fynbos area is that they too

may well invade the natural flora just as their hosts have done. In the case of the hakea, and some invasive acacias, extensive tests were done with the Australian long-snouted beetle that feeds off the fruit of the plants, to check that it did not develop a taste for the fynbos before setting it free in the Cape mountains. One of the reasons that the Australian plants such as acacias and hakeas fare so well against the local flora is that they were introduced here without their associated predators such as insects, fungi and rodents which would consume their fruits and seed banks. In Australia there is a similar problem with proteas and other plants introduced from the Cape.

The 'fynbos' heathlands of the Fynbos Biome (a term used to describe the Cape Floral Kingdom's ecological status) may not harbour the most typical Mediterranean flora, but certainly the most spectacular. 'Fynbos' is found on typically sandy, acidic soils, with a low level of nutrients, derived from the widespread TMS and more recent coastal sands. The biome is a nutrient-poor environment as the sand is not only marine in origin, but it has been severely leached over three million years of heavy winter rainfall. Most of the nutrients found in the system are held in the plants themselves rather than in the soil. But still, as anyone who has been there will know, the vegetation is generally too poor to sustain large animals. Even though big game was found at the Cape by early settlers, numbers were low.

The Renosterveld, named after the plant *Elytropappus rhinocerotis*, stretches over more fertile, clayey soils derived from granite and shale parent rock, but even this is a degraded veld type, having replaced grass and trees mainly through veld burning and overgrazing. Because the Renosterveld naturally occupies the more fertile valleys and plains, it in turn has been replaced by agriculture and urban expansion and only about nine per cent of the original veld remains. The Strandveld is the most typically Mediterranean vegetation of the Cape and it grows on coastal soils usually rich in calcium and with a low acidity. This veld type has a high component of Karoo succulents and it blends into the succulent Karoo veld type

Left: *The tablecloth of cloud over Table Mountain and the Twelve Apostles is a sure sign that summer's blustery south-easterly wind is blowing. While the wind desiccates plants and animals at lower altitudes, the mists and clouds which it spreads over the mountains bring much needed moisture there during the long Mediterranean summers.*

Above: *A Cape sugarbird* (Promerops cafer) *perches on a pincushion bush* (Leucospermum cordifolium), *eager for the plant's energy-giving nectar.*

Right: *The feet of rock hyraxes, or dassies, are kept moist by the secretions of glandular tissue in the thinly padded soles, enabling these small mammals to scuttle swiftly over precipitous rocky areas.*

along the north-western margin of the fynbos where it is called Sandveld.

The fynbos has had to survive the most stressful of conditions. Summers are dry and can become scorchingly hot, with the relentless south-east wind sucking moisture out of every pore and dessicating both plants and animals. Winters, on the other hand, can bring snow and frequent week-long rain storms that leave the soil waterlogged for most of the season. Yet some of the most beautiful plants in this floral paradise are to be found in the remotest, harshest places among the high, jagged mountain peaks. The marsh rose, *Orothamnus zeyheri*, for instance, grows only on the highest ridges of the Hottentots-Holland Mountains. Not long ago it was thought to have become extinct, until a fire in the Kogelberg area germinated a small, dormant seed bank of the plants and today they have been cultivated at Kirstenbosch National Botanical Gardens, saving it from possible extinction.

Fire is one of the anomalies of the Cape flora, for it seems that the vegetation is adapted to it, but like most things, too much is as bad as too little. Many fynbos plants have evolved physiological and

---

Left: *As the renosterveld habitat of the geometric tortoise* (Psammobates geometricus) *receded in the south-western Cape coastal area under pressure from agriculture, so the numbers of this now-endangered species decreased drastically. Several small reserves for these attractive reptiles have been set aside in surviving patches of renosterveld at Worcester, Wolseley, Paarl and Gordon's Bay.*
Above: *In the typical mountain fynbos region of the Kleinmond Nature Reserve, the 'coca-cola' colour of the Palmiet River is caused by humic acids leached out of the decaying vegetation in the upper layers of the coarse, acidic soils. In the days of the Cape Colony, black ink was made by boiling the leaves of the waboom tree* (Protea nitida) *with rusty iron, such as an old nail, and sugar.*

C·A·P·E F·L·O·R·A·L K·I·N·G·D·O·M

The word 'fynbos' is derived from the old Dutch *fijnbosch*, which was used to describe the fine-leaved plants, such as ericas, which are typical of the Western Cape's natural vegetation. Through common usage this term is now used to describe the vegetation which covers the mountains and coastal plains of the western and southern Cape.

However, many of the plants which grow in the so-called fynbos region are broad-leaved shrubs, such as taaibos (*Rhus* spp.)

and proteas, dune milkwoods and various small trees. The region is more correctly known as the Cape Floral Kingdom.

Ecologists refer to this area as the Fynbos Biome, because the ericoid fynbos is its most characteristic floral element. But fynbos is also found throughout the higher mountain regions of southern and eastern Africa, which is an ideal habitat for plants that are adapted to stressed and variable conditions. It would be correct to call the plants of the Cape Floral

Kingdom evergreen sclerophyllous shrubs.

More than anything it is the region's winter rainfall regime that determines its climate, the associated Mediterranean-type flora and the animals that can survive these unusual conditions, but it is the complexity of the landscape combined with nutrient-poor soils that has led evolution up such a wonderful and exuberant garden path. The Cape Peninsula, for example, is only about the size of the Isle of Wight, and yet it contains

about 2 000 plant species, a greater number of species than occurs in the entire British Isles. Some 8 500 plant species occur in the Cape Floral Kingdom as a whole and of these about 5 800 are endemic. The general species richness of the region, especially the great number of endemic species, has led botanists to classify it a distinct floral kingdom.

Many of the species found in the region occupy only a small area, sometimes being known from only a few communities, or in some cases a single community. Obviously such plants are extremely vulnerable and indeed the entire Cape flora may be considered to be endangered. The Hottentots-Holland Mountains which separate the Peninsula from the immediate hinterland contain perhaps the richest flora in all the world, with a profusion of flowering plants that for centuries has awed botanists and delighted mountaineers.

There are 21 species of subtly-shaded gladiolus found in these mountains, many types of orchids such as the red disa (*Disa uniflora*), blue disa (*Herschelia graminifolia*) and the 'moederkappie' (*Disperis capensis*).

Left above: *The rich Cape flora has been afforded the status of a distinct floral kingdom (of which there are six in the world) on account of the astonishing diversity of its flowering plants. Delicate blooms of the world-renowned chincherinchee (Ornithogalum thyrsoides) can be seen in the Cape mountains in early summer.*
Left: *In the Fernkloof Nature Reserve, the three main elements of the Cape Floral Kingdom are evident, namely the larger protea bushes, smaller erica bushes and reed-like restio plants.*
Above: *Most species of erica have vivid, bell-shaped flowers, much like this* Erica versicolor. *The leaves of these plants are small and tightly rolled to avoid loss of water during the Western Cape's rainless summers.*

Left: *Early white settlers, who were astonished by the Cape's botanical beauty, called the gorgeous* Gladiolus ornatus *'painted ladies'.*
Above: Dilatris pillansii *has an iron-based, haemoglobin-like compound which colours its roots blood-red.*
Far right below: *The ericoid leaves of the fountain bush (*Psoralea pinnata*) are typical of those plants of the Cape Floral Kingdom which give rise to the descriptive name of 'fynbos'.*

Right below: *Everlastings, such as these white* Helichrysum vestitum *and cerise* Phaenocoma prolifera *decorate all of Africa's highlands.*
Right above: *Although not as showy as the ericas or proteas, the reed-like restios, such as* Elegia juncea, *belong to one of the families which are most characteristic of the mountain fynbos communities.*

Here too can be found the grandest flower in all the fynbos, the king protea (*Protea cynaroides*), the velvety pink *Protea compacta*, the sugarbush (*P. neriifolia*) and milk-white *P. lacticolor*, squadrons of leucadendrons (cone bushes) and leucospermums (pincushions), lobelias, watsonias, 26 species of sorrel (*Oxalis*) that are harbingers of winter, over 200 varieties of ericas of every shape and colour imaginable, gorgeous irises, such as moraeas, and fields of scarlet, mauve or purple watsonias. The showy *Mimetes* genus also occurs here, such as *M. argenteus* whose soft red and yellow flowers flare out between tight clusters of silvery leaves. Carolus Linnaeus, the indefatigable 18th-century scientist who devised the modern binomial system of taxonomy, called the Cape 'that paradise on earth'. It was he who named the genus *Protea* after the Greek god Proteus who could appear in any number of guises.

The Cape Floral Kingdom is defined by a temperate, winter rainfall climate, enclosed by ocean and semi-arid land which is typical of all Mediterranean climatic regions. Its vegetation is characterized more by its evergreen shrublands than the better-known heathlands of ericas and restios with scattered bushes or clusters of protea trees. The

Above: *South Africa's national flower, Protea cynaroides or king protea, is found throughout the Cape Fold mountains, from sea level to above 1 500 metres. This plant thrives in coarse, acidic and nutritionally poor soil.*

Right above: *One of the rarest and most endangered plants of the Cape Floral Kingdom is the marsh rose, Orothamnus zeyheri. It was thought the plant had become extinct soon after it was described in 1848 by the German botanist, Karl Pappe. Sixty years later, some of these proteas were found on sale in Cape Town's flower market and traced back to their exposed mountain sanctuary. The only known communities grow in the protected Kogelberg area between Sir Lowry's Pass and Hermanus.*

tightly folded ericoid leaves of the heathland component are adapted to reduce water loss caused by the searing summer winds, and so they have become hard and leathery, often with hairy surfaces, or small and tightly rolled. These plants, called sclerophylls, contain chemicals which also help reduce water loss. (The leaves of plants in the arid biome of the sub-continent also contain these chemicals.) The plants are usually evergreen, to take advantage of optimal growing conditions which usually occur during spring and autumn.

Mediterranean conditions are found, naturally enough, around the Mediterranean Sea but also along the south-western margin of Australia, the mid-western coastal strip of South America, the coastal districts of southern California and of course at the south-

western tip of Africa. Although these areas are geographically and biologically widely separated, the plants all look surprisingly similar. It is the similar climates and resulting environmental stresses in these areas that have driven their individual floras to adopt the same functions and similar forms in order to survive. The phenomenon of such unrelated and geographically distant organisms coming to resemble each other in appearance and function is called convergent evolution; stand in any Mediterranean-type landscape and you will be surprised just how alike they look.

Below: Erica grandiflora *is one of the more than 400 erica species found in the Fynbos Biome.*

behavioural mechanisms to withstand fires, such as thick, fire-resistant bark or growing-stocks situated below ground so that they re-shoot after a fire. Geophytic or bulbous plants, such as watsonias, may only shoot after fire has swept the area. But in the case of seeding proteas, for instance - which although they may be adapted to fire and only release their seeds after burning - a second fire may destroy new plants before they have reached maturity and have been able to produce new seed.

Foresters use fire to keep the fynbos healthy, but there is much controversy about the optimal period between burns. The foresters

Above: *Below the imposing Langeberge lies the Bontebok National Park. This park was set up specifically to protect the endangered bontebok and has succeeded admirably. Surplus animals have been used to establish other herds, notably in De Hoop Nature Reserve at Bredasdorp, and the Cape of Good Hope Nature Reserve at Cape Point.*

usually burn the fynbos at seven- to 12-year intervals to maintain steady water yields, but many farmers shorten the intervals considerably to produce better grazing. Some ecologists believe that if left unburned, the fynbos will succeed to forest and there is some evidence to support these claims, at least where rainfall is high enough. At Jonkershoek near Stellenbosch and Orange Kloof near Cape Town there are patches of fynbos which have not been burned for over 40 years. Rather than becoming moribund and choked, as was generally thought to be the inevitable course of events, they appear to be tending to forest. Another example of the tendency can be seen in Bain's Kloof, where waboom (*Protea nitida*) grow 20 metres tall.

The general absence of trees in the Fynbos Biome is another point of controversy which has only recently been suitably explained. In the mountain kloofs Afro-montane forest patches are usually found, while along rivers and in other sheltered rocky areas trees like the *Euclea*, wild olive, *Rhus* and *Heeria* genera are found.

ern Africa and over 200 are found between the Hottentots-Holland Mountains and Hermanus on the coast. Finally there are the proteas, of which the famous protea flowers make up only one of many genera; others of the Proteaceae family are the pincushions, cone bushes, *Mimetes*, the rare marsh rose, *Brabejum stellatifolium* - the bitter almond tree used by Jan van Riebeeck for his famous hedge in Kirstenbosch that defined the colony's early border (some of the original trees are still growing there) - and the genus *Faurea* which includes the Transvaal boekenhout tree.

This fynbos vegetation is not confined to the Cape Floral Kingdom, but follows the high ground of the Escarpment and other mountains all the way up into East Africa. This tropical affinity of the Cape's vegetation leads ecologists to the conclusion that the fynbos did not originate from its current range but that it is tropically derived. Shifting climatic conditions have isolated the Capensis flora from its genetic source, and Mediterranean conditions over the past few thousand years have driven the mechanisms of convergent evolution to suit local conditions.

Nothing in nature remains static, and there is a continual process at work in all flora called 'succession'. Vegetation responds to climatic changes and varying nutrient regimes in the environment and also, over the past 10 000 years or so, to man's interference with nature. Given the right conditions, it seems that all other vegetation types will succeed to forest. The elements that define the direction and rate of succession are the availability of nutrients and moisture; where both of these elements are reduced the fynbos tends towards a succulent flora which in turn will succeed to desert, as it does towards the Namib. When both elements are found in abundance the fynbos will tend to temperate forest, as it does in the southern Cape around Knysna. When nutrients are abundant but moisture is low the fynbos succeeds to a Karoo-type flora and as moisture increases (given high nutrient status) Karoo becomes Strandveld, Strandveld becomes savanna or Renosterveld if disturbed, and then finally forest.

The fynbos area is noted more for its flora than its animals, as the nutrient-poor environment that has produced an extraordinary diversity of flowering plants is low in actual output. Of course, there are many creatures that have evolved in, or adapted to this environment and most impressive perhaps are the small colourful birds that thrive on the rich nectar produced by each spring eruption of flowers. Cape sugarbirds seem to stick to the glazed leucospermum beads and the sugarbush flowers; malachite, collared and orange-breasted sunbirds twitter and flit among the ericas and proteas, their long, curved beaks probing the blooms. Ground woodpeckers and Cape rock-jumpers are familiar residents of the mid slopes of the mountains where black harriers glide close to the ground, exciting the tiny, shy cisticolas and warblers that hide in the low scrub. Migratory steppe buzzards seem to occupy every available telephone pole through the spring and summer, their dull brown colour well suited to the wheatlands around Swellendam which host the rodents they eat.

The most impressive mammal of the fynbos is the Cape mountain leopard. It is the same species (*Panthera pardus*) as the other southern African leopard but is generally smaller than specimens from the Transvaal Lowveld, for example. It was once thought that there were only a few left in the wild mountain areas, but studies using radio-tracking equipment have shown them to be fairly numerous, with huge, overlapping territories. Although numerous only in the mountains, these leopards are nevertheless still shot, trapped and poisoned by farmers who in the process often kill jackals, wild cats, the harmless aardwolf and many birds of prey which in no way threaten livestock. (In 1987 two leopards were seen on

Although there is reason to accept that trees would have difficulty surviving on the higher mountains, one would expect to find more trees in the shrublands. The reason for the paucity here is now believed to be a result of over-frequent veld burning by hunter-gatherers during the past 10 000 years, to promote the shooting of geophytes, an important food source, and grass to attract game. Later the veld was burned by Hottentot and white pastoralists to provide grazing for their flocks and herds and to open the shrublands for agriculture.

Although the Cape Floral Kingdom contains a staggering variety of plants, three families are used to define and describe it. The most important and widespread family is the Restionaceae, which is made up of reed-like plants such as the *Restio*, *Elegia* and *Thamnochortus* genera. The restios have separate male and female plants and they are most common in the mountainous areas. Next are the ericas whose bell-shaped flowers light up the folded mountains in spring. There are 663 species of erica, 636 of which occur in south-

numerous occasions in the public resort areas around Cape Hang-klip on the eastern tip of False Bay. One was promptly shot by a local farmer but the other vanished back into the wilds. These two leopards may have been hunting seabirds or fish from the rock pools for, although they will eat livestock, dogs and even baboons, they also eat insects, birds, reptiles and fish.) Many species of game, such as lion, elephant, hippos and buffalo were found in limited numbers in the Cape, but, like the bloubok and quagga of the interior, they were soon exterminated in this region by the fire power, the fear and the greed of southern Africa's early white colonists.

One of the larger animals occurring in the fynbos is the bonte-bok (*Damaliscus dorcas dorcas*). The species came perilously close to joining the bloubok in extinction, through relentless hunting. The establishment of the Bontebok National Park near Swellendam has ensured its present survival, but the species suffers generally from infestation by parasites and weakened bones due to the general deficiency of minerals in the fynbos. Trace minerals such as copper are supplemented by salt licks in the park as well as in the Cape Point Nature Reserve where other herds are conserved. Another reserve has been set aside in the Fynbos Biome to protect the rarest of all southern African tortoises, the geometric tortoise, so named for the geometric yellow-and-black patterns on its shell. It is a small but attractive reptile that inhabits the coastal Renosterveld near Cape Town, Gordon's Bay and Paarl. It also occurs in the north-western portion of the region, as far up as Piketberg. This is a wheat-growing area, known as the Swartland, where intense cultivation of the rich granite- and shale-derived soils has destroyed the habitat of the geometric tortoise, as has the proliferation of vineyards in the other parts of its range. Some of the plant species, too, are in danger of extinction. In an ecotone between Renosterveld and Strandveld in the Joostenberg area near Paarl, the last remaining community of *Leucodendron verticillatum* is fenced off. But even the electrified fence which was used to protect the community of marsh roses on the Kogelberg was not enough to keep out greedy collectors, who burrowed under it to steal the plants.

It has recently been discovered that ants play a vital role in the survival of many fynbos plants. In a process called myrmecochory, the ants carry seeds back to their nests to eat the fleshy, oily attachments to the seeds called elaiosomes. The seeds are then discarded in the nutrient-enriched nests or ant middens - their rubbish dumps - where the seeds germinate close to the surface. This process obviously provides a competitive advantage for both ants and seedlings in a nutrient-poor environment. The seeds of about 1 300 types of restios, grasses, proteas and other species, in fact about 20 per cent of Cape flora, are dispersed in this way. This short-distance dispersal, coupled with a general lack of long-distance dispersal mechanisms, helps to explain the high degree of endemism of the fynbos, as there is limited gene flow between plant communities.

Unfortunately another alien infestation, this time by the aggressive Argentine ant (*Iridomyrmex humilis*), threatens to oust indigenous ants from fynbos areas and this in turn threatens the survival of myrmecochorous plants. These invading ants, which are thought to have been introduced to the area in imported horse feed during the South African War (1899 - 1902), also eat the elaiosome

Left: *The scourge of sheep and poultry farmers in the Cape and elsewhere, the caracal is a handsome, nocturnal cat. Its natural prey consists of game-birds, dassies, ground squirrels and small antelope.*

Above: *Because of its low nutrient status, the Fynbos Biome cannot support much wildlife, and it is relatively poor in bird species. Nectar-sipping birds, such as this malachite sunbird, however, benefit from the profusion of flowering plants, and especially from the various proteaceous sugarbushes.*

but do not bury the seeds, so that they lie on the surface of the ground to be eaten by birds and mice.

The Cape Floral Kingdom occupies only one per cent of southern Africa, yet it has over 60 per cent of endangered plant species of the sub-continent. Two-thirds of its natural range has been overrun by agriculture and urban expansion and what remains is mainly the Mountain Fynbos which, while being fascinating for its unusual and prolific flowering plants, is the least productive part of the biome - which is exactly why it has been left more or less intact. The need for water and the construction of dams and high level reservoirs in mountain valleys for hydro-electric power are, however, now beginning to threaten parts of even this environment. Disregarding the timber plantations, it has been estimated that 24 per cent of the remaining Fynbos Biome has been invaded by woody alien species. From this it would seem that a bleak future awaits the world's smallest and richest floral kingdom, one that has inestimable aesthetic and scientific value, as well as great economic value. As in all ecosystems, its survival is necessary for the survival of all its inhabitants. If anything, it will be the wildflower industry of the fynbos area and its potential for high quality water yield that will ensure its conservation and ultimate survival.

Left: *Rock pigeons are as at home nesting in mountains or forests as they are in town gardens or even city centres. In the urban environment they mix with feral pigeons and occasionally mate with them and produce hybrid offspring.*
Top: *Grysbok are still found in the Cape Peninsula, close to built-up areas. They prefer to lie up during the day in thick scrub in fynbos communities, and emerge to feed on grass and the leaves of small bushes at night. They are sometimes a nuisance in vineyards as they will eat the young leaves and fruit with relish.*
Above: *Perhaps the most interesting but least known of the fynbos fauna are the insects, such as the green stick insect* (Macynia labiata) *whose camouflage makes it hard to see among stems.*

The Arid West

THE EARTH'S CRUST IS MADE UP of numerous large and small plates which we see as continents or parts of continents. At one time all the southern continents, plus India and Arabia, formed a giant continent that has been called Gondwanaland. About 200 million years ago Gondwanaland began to fracture owing to widespread volcanic activity, forcing the separate plates to drift away from one another on the earth's semi-liquid mantle.

About 85 million years ago, Africa and South America parted company, with convection cells under the newly-formed Atlantic Ocean spewing out lava along the Mid-Atlantic Ridge and increasing the area of the sea bed. With no land masses to impede its flow, the West Wind Drift current churned around the Southern Ocean, as it still does. An offshoot of this current found its way up between the two newly formed continents. Water from the Antarctic also flowed northwards between Africa and South America, and the combined flow of water from these two sources resulted in the cold Benguela Current. The air mass above this cold current too was cooled, setting up the South Atlantic high pressure atmospheric system that is characterized by strong, descending winds.

Under these conditions little vapour is able to rise from the sea and few clouds dimple the sky, but on most mornings dense fog banks envelope a narrow strip of coastline up to 50 kilometres wide, as if to tease the land. With little rain, no permanent rivers or lakes and only the relentless topical sun to nurture it, the south-western margin of Africa has grown steadily more and more arid. While the local climates of today's arid western zone have fluctuated widely over the past 85 million years, the unforgiving desert that marks the coastline between the Cunene and Orange rivers has been a constant presence.

The arid west includes the full extents of the Desert and Succulent Karoo Biomes, the north-western part of the Nama-Karoo Biome, as well as the south-western part of the Kalahari. This is the area approximately west of the 250-millimetre isohyet (a line connecting all places of equal annual rainfall). Plant geographers call it the Karoo-Namib region, for although it includes all or parts of four biomes, many plants are widespread throughout the the the whole area and adaptations to very low rainfalls are common throughout. The word 'desert' is derived from Latin and means a forsaken place or wasteland, while 'Karoo' is a Hottentot word that refers to the semi-deserts of south-western South Africa. The only perennial rivers of this entire area are the Orange, its tributary the Fish, and the Olifants River which all rise in mountains far beyond margins of the arid zone.

The arid west is characterized largely by the strong development of its succulent flora, which is the most common floral adaptation to cope with the stresses of heat and aridity. There are two basic survival strategies employed by the flora of this zone, the first being drought tolerance, typical of the semi-desert regions. Common drought tolerant adaptations are the fleshy leaves and stems of succulent plants; and geophytic plants, which store their mois-

---

Left: *Signpost to the western wastelands - a bleached gemsbok skeleton.*

109

Above: *Nara melons are an important source of water and food for gemsbok in the Namib Desert.*

Right: *Gemsbok are perhaps the best-adapted large inhabitants of the Namib. The glossy silver-grey coat protects the skin from the sun's radiation and reflects a large amount of heat back into the atmosphere. Even so, during the day the body temperature of a gemsbok may be as high as 45 ^{o} C; as blood warmer than 42 ^{o} C will cause permanent brain damage, how is it possible for the antelope to move about all day in search of juicy nara melons? Beneath a gembok's black muzzle markings, there is a network of fine capillaries in which venous blood is cooled by the animal's heavy breathing. This blood then moves into an organ below the brain where it cools the hotter arterial blood by up to 3 ^{o} C on its way from the heart to the brain.*

ture and nutrients safely underground. The other strategy is drought avoidance which is more typical of the true desert plants. Drought avoidance may be achieved through ephemeral growth and seeding directly after rains, by plants being able to absorb moisture from the atmosphere or by having extensive tap and lateral root systems. The *Stipagrostis* and *Aristida* grasses of the Namib dune desert have lateral roots that can extend up to 20 metres from the grass stems. The roots help to anchor the grass to its inconstant world and the root hairs are able to absorb even the minutest amount of dew that condenses from coastal fogs. Research with rye plants has shown that the total length of root hairs from a single plant may be well over 10 000 kilometres.

The spiky nara butternut (*Acanthosicyos horrida*) is a xerophytic plant that reduces water loss in the scorching Namib dunes by not having any leaves, its spines taking over the function of photosynthesis. It grows in the dune area south of the Kuiseb River where the

plants are prone to become covered by the shifting sands, but this doesn't deter the nara melon. When the parent becomes inundated with sand it sends out lateral stems, and where these emerge from the dunes they take root to form new plants, always keeping one step ahead of the marching dunes. The succulent, spiky fruit is an important source of food and water for gemsbok, and often the only food available to the Topnaar Hottentots who live along the Kuiseb's dry river bed.

On one's first visit to the Namib it is surprising to see a lone gemsbok kicking up a thin line of dust as it trudges through the dunes in terrible afternoon heat searching for nara melons, or a small herd of elephants drifting across the gnarled Kaokoveld, grey spectres on seas of sand and stone. But mammals are able to regulate their body temperatures, giving off heat and water through breathing and sweating. The larger the animal the smaller will be its surface area relative to its mass, and so the less water it will need to thermoregulate, compared with smaller animals. An elephant or rhino needs to lose somewhere around 1,5 per cent of its body weight every hour in order to maintain a constant body temperature of 40°C. A dune-living gerbil or mole, however, will need to lose about 20 per cent of its body weight every hour to maintain the same body temperature, which is why you will not see them out in the midday sun.

There are three main ecosystems within the Namib Desert, the largest of which are the gravel plains that lie between the Kuiseb and Cunene rivers and the moon-like landscapes of the Kaokoveld, where the pale pink quartzitic and grey granite outcrops are run through by bands of black dolerite. South of the Kuiseb River is the sand sea, an area where the blanched calcrete plains have been covered by shifting orange dunes. These dune sands are derived from the submarine Orange River delta and returned to the sea by the Kuiseb River. The Kuiseb River seldom flows, but when it does it comes down in a churning, frothy sludge carrying with it the sand that has accumulated in its dry bed since the previous surface flow. This demarcation between the gravel plains and the sand sea is the clearest feature that one sees in a satellite image of the area, and it highlights the importance of the third ecosystem, the dry river beds.

Major drainage channels are not considered to be part of the Desert Biome, as they are corridors with a higher moisture regime which allow for the migration of plants and animals of the Savanna Biome to penetrate into the the heart of the desert. These linear oases are the arteries carrying life-sustaining nutrients and moisture to the Namib and even in the driest years animals know where to find water in the sandy canyon channels. Large acacia trees grow in river beds and smaller trees and bushes provide food and shelter for weavers and doves, owls and eagles, while the flowers of wild tobacco plants and aloes attract sunbirds and butterflies. Game comes to graze the ostrich grass and browse on the bushes, and always close behind will be spotted hyaenas and lappet-faced vultures.

Just before it flies back to roost in a large camel thorn tree that grows in the Kuiseb Canyon, a spotted eagle owl (*Bubo africanus*) swoops silently over the dunes to catch itself a meal. This may consist of a sidewinding adder, one *Aporosaura* lizard, perhaps three tenebrionid beetles, a cricket, a few termites and a small amount of half-digested dry grass and lichen. Of course, it gets this gourmet's delight by eating just the one adder, which was caught out hunting lizards. The lizards had been hunting before dawn for beetles that had been out to drink fog dew, and so on. The eagle owl may decide that a smaller barn owl (*Tyto alba*) is a more tasty breakfast than a snake, in which case its breakfast will include the golden mole, a few gerbils, a grey musk shrew or perhaps a round-eared elephant shrew, maybe even a Smith's rock elephant-shrew and a striped

Above: *On hot, windless days in the Namib Desert, ostriches are able to cool off by running with their wings slightly lifted and their feathers fanned out. They eat almost anything found on the ground, from grass seeds to succulent plants and small reptiles.*

Right: *Many theories have been proposed concerning the behaviour and coloration of tenebrionid beetles of the Namib. Earlier theories of the beetles' shading one another during feeding proved to be inaccurate observations of their attempts to mate. It was formerly thought that the white carapaces of some species were an adaptation for the reflection of heat. Since most heat is derived from surface reflection and convection, and not from direct radiation, it appears that this is not necessarily the case. Also, some carapaces are white, while others are yellow or orange or even black.*

mouse that the barn owl had caught in a good night's hunting.

Dawn breaks over the distant eastern mountains, etched in dark blue tones against the seeping light, and burnishing the dunes

in a glowing bronze light. In one morning out of three the desert wakes up in a shroud of cool fog draped across the dunes, highlighting the deep indigo shadows of their curvilinear crests before dissipating in shredded sheets on the gravel plains some 50 kilometres inland. The moisture condenses on the cold ground and plants, wetting their surfaces, while dew drops slide down grass stems and drip onto the sand.

Onymacris unguicularis is a large tenebrionid beetle that is usually active on wind-cooled days, eating organic detritis that collects along the bases of the dunes. When dew begins to collect on the dune surface, however, the beetle awakens in the dark like a reluctant worker and trudges up the steep slip face of the dune to where condensation is greatest. Once on the cold crest, *Onymacris* turns its head into the wind and raises its carapace like a shield on which the fog condenses. The drops run slowly down the beetle's shell and drip into its open mouth. Some of these tenebroinids, such as *Onymacris bicolor*, have evolved extremely long legs to keep them above the scorching dune sands as they go foraging for detritus.

Lack of water is the most critical limiting factor of the desert and especially in the seemingly-barren lines of dunes that reach up to 300 metres above the ground. But a closer look reveals the dunes to be dotted with tufts of short grass, like the stubble on an unshaven face. The fog moisture that keeps the plants alive is not enough to coax their seeds into germination, but a few days after even a light drizzle the sand sea can be transformed into a swaying green grassland. All the available moisture and energy is used to produce seeds so that when the plants wither and die, the light, aerodynamic seeds are picked up and spread about by the wind.

The wind which shapes the dunes is also the provider of food in the sand sea, for dead grass is really the basis of the food chain here. Beetles and ants, dune larks and ostriches eat the seeds and detritus that the wind blows around the dune corridors, collecting it along the bases of the dunes. Like other desert birds, ostriches can regulate their body temperatures by thermal panting. Their feathers act as an insulator against excessive sunshine and they can be raised off their backs to assist heat loss by convection. When there is a wind,

the raised feathers allow air to move freely across their skin to draw off body fluid and cool the bird. The feathers are later flattened against the skin to keep in body heat once the sun drops like a melting coin into western ocean, for without a vegetable gown, the ground quickly loses its heat to the atmosphere. These birds are not confined to any one habitat and range freely across the arid region.

Ironically, it is the lack of water in the desert that leads to availability of the all-important detritus, for without water there are no fungi and bacteria to decompose the dry grass. The wind and fog of the desert are also the providers of lichen, which grow on the gravel plains where they absorb fog moisture. Lichens can withstand extreme climatic conditions but they are extremely sensitive to unnatural disturbances. When a vehicle leaves the road in the Namib it kills large numbers of the lichens which sustain the herds of springbok on the plains. The wind carries dislodged lichen into the dune fields where it joins the detritus food chain. Herds of springbok survive on the Namib's gravel plains, existing mostly on lichens. They never have to drink and can obtain all their body fluids from their food, either from the fog moisture absorbed by the lichen or through the digestive process.

Plants such as *Welwitschia mirabilis* can absorb fog moisture directly through leaves, passing water down to their roots. When, in 1860, Friedrich Welwitsch first laid eyes on this plant growing on the stony desert floor, he is said to have fallen to his knees and marvelled, sure that he was looking at the most majestic creation that tropical Africa had to offer. This plant is one of the Namib's unique creations, having the characteristics of both gymnosperms (cone-bearing plants) and angiosperms (flowering plants); it is of special scientific interest as it is thought to be an evolutionary bridge between the two groups. Some of these living plants are around 2 000 years old and they have only two leathery, sclerophyllous leaves which grow throughout their lives. One wonders how long these would be if they did not die back during dry years and were not shredded by sand-blasting winds or chewed by game for moisture.

Depressions which collect rain water become focal points of desert life, attracting animals and birds from afar. One of the com-

Left: *The elephants that wander along the Ugab and Hoanib rivers in the Skeleton Coast Park in the Kaokoveld must travel vast distances to find food and water. A fully grown bull elephant eats about 250 kilograms of food a day. When the rivers dry up completely, the elephants use their tusks to dig in the river beds until the water-table is reached. Water is a by-product of digestion so desert elephants can last for a few days at a time without drinking.*

Above: *The side-winding adder (*Bitis peringueyi*) also collects fog dew on its body, sliding its mouth across its scales to suck up the cool liquid, but it obtains about 75 per cent of its moisture from eating lizards and spiders. The adder frequents the inter-dune corridors, submerging itself in the soft sand hummocks that collect around plants by performing quick, lateral, S-shaped movements. Its eyes are situated on the top of its head and only these protrude above the sand as it waits in ambush. Geckos and shovel-snouted lizards are attracted by little flicks of the adder's tail, which they mistake for an insect. But if a beetle-engorged shovel-snouted lizard (*Aporosaura anchietae*) does not happen along, a gecko-stuffed dancing white lady spider (*Leucorchestris sp.*) will do. The adder moves with a side-winding motion that allows it to traverse the loose dune slip faces with minimum contact but maximum friction.*

Right: *The red Kalahari dunes derive their colour from ferrous minerals in the sand. The colour deepens the further one moves inland away from the pale coastal dunes.*

mon visitors to these transient pans are sandgrouse, which fly long distances every few days to reach water. They arrive in relayed flocks, landing a few metres from the water's edge and then advance in squadrons, each drinking for less than a minute before taking off in a sudden blur of beating wings. Sandgrouse have downy chest feathers which absorb liquid. When the birds arrive back at their nests, the chicks can drink by sucking the water-laden feathers of the parent birds.

Small bands of Topnaar Hottentots live in the Namib, herding their goats along the Kuiseb Canyon and collecting nara melons in the dunes. Hunter - gatherers have lived in the desert for at least

8 000 years, for that is the maximum age of nara melon seeds recovered from archaeological sites in the area. But most of what we know about the Namib's ecology has been painstakingly collected by scientists living at the Namib Research Institute at Gobabeb near the edge of the Kuiseb Canyon. Doubts are often raised about the relevance of scientific research that looks at obscure details like the digestive enzymes of dune beetles, but to use a familiar technological metaphor, it is precisely this kind of specialized research that helps us to understand the workings of the biotic machine, its forces and fuels, its materials and mechanics.

Humans tampering with natural ecosystems have been

likened to cave men and women with crude stone tools, sitting in the dust and gazing idiot-like at a dismantled clock as they try to figure out how to reassemble the pieces without even knowing what the thing is supposed to do. When modern man's bulldozers and ploughs, his dams and highways disturb the natural biotic machinery, it is the mechanics at places like Gobabeb to which we must turn to help us repair the damage.

In the winter rainfall area of the Succulent Karoo Biome, nature has been given the chance to create a splendid profusion of plants which delights botanists but confounds the taxonomists who try to identify and describe the explosion of succulent flora that has

evolved here. A rule of nature seems to be that nothing succeeds like proliferation, so while the climate of the Succulent Karoo encourages survival strategies, a predictable rainfall of 200 millimetres or less a year allows for this proliferation to occur, albeit of small and sometimes bizarre growth forms. The phenomenal speciation of this specialized semi-desert flora is similar to that of the neighbouring fynbos flora, both being winter rainfall areas with dystrophic (nutrient-poor) soils.

The biome extends from the coast-hugging strip of the Namib Desert, southwards from the Orange River to its meeting with the fynbos region, and it then turns inland behind the Cedarberg Mountains into the Taqua Karoo and along the valleys of the Langeberg and Swartberg mountain ranges to form the Little Karoo. The succulent Karoo is confined to the valley floors among the inland Cape Fold mountains at altitudes below 600 metres, above which the increased precipitation allows fynbos to flourish.

In one tropical family alone, the Mesembryanthemaceae, over 2000 species have been recorded in South Africa and still the list is incomplete. Like the mesems, or 'vygies' as they are more commonly called, the crassulas are another cosmopolitan family which in the Succulent Karoo Biome have undergone great diversification. The family name means 'thick' and refers to the bunched, overlapping leaves of the plump plants. Some are tiny plants that show the typical overlapping leaf structure, but being so small they resemble the stone flowers (*Lithops*) and unless in flower they are hard to see against the stony ground. This family includes the squat 'botterboom' (*Cotyledon paniculata*) whose distribution exactly fits the domain of the Succulent Karoo.

Stapelias and euphorbias, on the other hand, have large fleshy stems filled with a watery or milky sap. The euphorbias include large tropical forest trees and tiny desert succulents, but perhaps best known species is the 'naboom' or candelabra tree (*E. ingens*) of the Bushveld.

The Nama Karoo Biome begins in the fire-tempered hills of

Left: *Herds of springbok survive on the Namib's gravel plains, existing mostly on lichen. They never have to drink and can obtain all their body fluids from their food, either from the fog moisture absorbed by the lichen or through the digestive process.*

Above: *Male* Welwitschia mirabilis *plants have small, red, cone-like flowers that look like cocktail sausages on sticks, while the female plants (seen here) have larger, blue-green cones that are pollinated by insects and arachnids, such as nectar-seeking flies and the crab spiders which trap them, and by the cotton-stainer bug* Odontopus sexpunctatus. *These yellow, black-spotted bugs spend their entire lives sheltered by and feeding off welwitschia plants; the red, black-spotted bug that is also seen on the plants is the larval form of* Odontopus. *Mature bugs mate tail to tail and can often be seen moving about the plant in this fashion, the larger female bug dictating the direction of travel. Fertile cones each produce about 100 winged seed-pods, but many of these are eaten by animals where they land or are infected by woolly mealy-bugs. But as part of this plant's private ecosystem, the mealy-bugs excrete a honey-like liquid which attracts pollinating insects, which in turn feed the spiders.*

Right: *The Cape red-tailed lizard (*Platysaurus capensis*) is a common inhabitant of the granite boulders around Augrabies Falls.*

northern Damaraland, where farms with names like Twyfelfontein (the spring of doubt) tell of its inconstant nature. It is a thin strip of land here, sandwiched between the Namib Desert to the west and the arid savanna of the Kalahari Basin to the east. This northern part of the biome is known locally by the self- explanatory name of the Pro-Namib.

In the lowland areas of Damaraland small succulent trees like the bottle-shaped *Pachypodium lealii* are found on the clinkered ground. It seems quite incongruous that such an awkward-looking tree, in such a jagged environment should bear such delicate white and purple flowers on the tips of its spindly branches. The tree also contains a deadly toxin that was used by the Bushmen in preparing their arrow poisons. Many plants in the arid region contain poisonous or bitter chemicals which protect them from herbivores which might otherwise over-exploit individual plants. Research has shown, however, that black rhinos of Damaraland are able to eat many of the plants which other animals avoid without showing ill effects.

The Nama Karoo Biome broadens southwards to include extensive areas of the Namibian plateau, the dry grasslands of the southern Kalahari and the dwarf shrublands of the Great Karoo. This is flat country with low, fringing hills, where most of the intermittent rivers are not bold enough to forge a way through to major drainage systems; they simply flow out across shallow depressions where they form large salt pans such as the Verneukpan complex near Kenhardt.

On the margin between the Nama and the Kalahari savanna lies Etosha Pan. This giant salt pan falls within the Savanna Biome, but its plants and its functioning are those of a dry grassland, where periodic flooding and the resulting brackish substrate have all but eliminated trees from the 6 000 square kilometre 'pan of dry waters'. The pan is part of the Etosha Pan National Park which in both area and the size of its game herds is enormous, even within the vast scale of Namibia. This pan, as well as the Makgadikgadi Salt Pans, Lake Ngami, Nxai Pan, Lake Xau and the Okavango Delta are the remains of the biggest lake ever known to have existed. But aeolian sands flowing into the Kalahari Basin slowly replaced its waters and bullied the Cunene, Zambezi and other vanished rivers into forging new drainage channels for themselves.

The marginal semi-desert areas are all potentially rich grasslands, but they cannot recover from overuse during regular dry periods, during which, in times past, the people would move off the land and give it time to recover. Even the annual spring shower of daisies that lights up the fields of Namaqualand is a spectacle that every year delights nature lovers, but it owes its brilliance in part to the degraded veld. These ephemeral flowers are designed to take advantage of transient conditions in marginal areas. Although they would naturally be there to bloom after the first rains of spring, when the land is disturbed they flourish as the first stage in recovering the natural climax vegetation.

Most of the flowers that set Namaqualand ablaze in springtime belong to the family *Asteraceae*, which is one of the largest flowering families on earth and includes the gazanias ('gousblomme'), ursinias (marigolds), *Euryops* genus (including the Clanwilliam daisy) and everlastings (*Helichrysum* sp.) which are more common in the Fynbos Biome and Afro-montane highlands.

To the west the land changes from Namaqualand's scrub semidesert to the southern Kalahari, which consists almost entirely of dune sands covered by *Stipagrostis* and similar sweet grasses and open acacia savanna. The Nossob and Auob are the two largest rivers of the southern Kalahari and although they stand dry for most of the year, like the rivers of the Namib, they are vital arteries of the

Above: ' *He comes only when the moon is dark, I hear his far-off call...' wrote the poet N.P. van Wyk Louw of the brown hyaena, likening it to the approach of death.*
Left: *Black or hook-lipped rhinoceroses still exist in small numbers in the Kaokoveld and Damaraland. Despite being protected animals, they are still poached by local tribesmen and rich white hunters. The rhinos eat mainly the juicy euphorbia plants which grow in the desert, and they seem to be unconcerned by the bitter chemicals which discourage other animals from eating these plants.*

N·A·M·A·Q·U·A·L·A·N·D

Left above: *Flowers such as Gazania lichtensteini appear in breathtaking profusion as a direct result of overgrazing. Their biological role is to help regenerate the tired veld and is the first step in plant succession. This succession tends towards a shrub-dominated flora, but in vain, for overgrazing is resumed as soon as the spring flowers show.*

Left below: *Although Namaqualand's flora exhibits several intriguing features to botanists, the main attraction for most people is the annual magnificent display of spring flowers.*

Below right and above: *The family Mesembryanthemaceae, represented here by M. crystallinum and Drosanthemum hispidum respectively, has over 2 000 recorded species - and this list is probably not yet complete.*

Below left: *An unexplained phenomenon, which intrigues botanists is the profusion and seemingly endless array of small succulent plant species on the Cape's north-western coast. Certain families of plants contain numerous species with complex relationships, which will take botanical taxonomists many years to unravel.*

The stapelias, such as Hoodia gordonii, *have evolved some of the most interesting reproductive architectures in the plant kingdom. Most of the flowers are large and fleshy, giving off a heavy foetid odour that attracts pollinating insects. The pollen is formed in two sacs with a connecting bridge which looks like a yolk. The bags attach themselves to the legs of insects and are then transported to other flowers of the same species, where they slot perfectly into the stigmatic grooves. The pollen bags and stigmas of each species have a precise key-and-lock fit.*

dual gemsbok game reserves of South Africa and Botswana. The river beds are wide and flat expanses of swaying grass for most of the year and lined with towering acacia trees. These trees provide roosting and nesting for the greatest concentration of raptors to be seen anywhere: lappet-faced vultures from as far away as the Namib come here to feed, martial eagles build their platform nests, tawny eagles and bateleurs, pigmy falcons, western red-footed kestrels and pale chanting goshawks all find a place to rest and to nest.

Through the long grass of the Kalahari's dry river beds the kori bustard (*Ardeotis kori*) strides confidently, swaying and bobbing slowly as it forages for just about any living thing to eat. This bustard's diet is as catholic as the ostrich's and, like the world's largest bird, it too has a claim to fame, being the heaviest flying bird.

Still moving to the south-east, the arid zone finally spills out across the Plains of Kamdeboo, the Great Karoo, where massive bands of dolerite form typical flat mountain ranges, the horizontal strata of the sediments of the Karoo geological sequence falling away in tiers to the dusty valleys of desolation and deception.

These mountains are part of the Karoo National Park where attempts are being made recreate the former splendour of this eco-system. The park lies in the heart of the country's sheep farming industry and conservationists hope, by re-establishing the tall grasslands of times past to convince farmers of the need for better veld management. The park provides the sanctuary for that scourge of sheep farmers, the caracal (*Felis caracal*) for there is apparently no compromise between the behaviour of this notoriously blood-frenzied predator and economic demands of farmers squeezing the most out of the tired land.

From the windswept summits of the Nuweveldberge, looking out across the plains of the Great Karoo to the folded range of the Swartberge in the hazy south, one can see the geological evidence of the passage of time. The Escarpment grassland plateau is referred to as a 'Gondwana' surface, whereas the intermittent dolerite steps and semi-desert plains between constitute an 'African' surface. The Gondwana surface dates from the time of the existence of the composite landmass of Gondwanaland; the African surfaces are the result of erosion that was unleashed when the southern super-continent broke up and Africa emerged. Wind and rain have been whittling away the high ground ever since. It is anticipated that all will eventually be reduced to a lower, African surface.

Far left: *A wild cat of the arid lands is the small spotted cat (Felis nigripes), more commonly called the black-footed cat. Sheep are far too large a prey for this small nocturnal predator, which prefers a diet of rodents and arachnids. Although they are known to be common in the arid areas of southern Africa, little is known about their behaviour.*

Left: *A common sight in large acacias and kokerbooms (Aloe dichotoma), as well as on the telephone poles that line roads, are the massive grass-ball condominiums of sociable weavers (Philetairus socius). Dozens of breeding pairs of these dull-coloured weavers communally build and inhabit these extraordinary structures, which sometimes become so heavy that they break the boughs which support them. Once the housing development is completed, other tenants await an opportunity to fill any vacant units; rosy-faced lovebirds are welcome guests, but eagle owls which roost on top of the weaver's nests lower the tone of the neighbourhood by feeding on their hosts. Even less welcome are the snakes which come to steal any unguarded eggs and nestlings. The ranges of both the kokerboom and sociable weaver quite accurately mirror that of the Nama floral domain.*

Below: *The scorpions of the arid west are generally more poisonous than those of other areas. Scorpions with thin tails and large pincers are less dangerous than the thick-tailed species which have small- to medium-size pincers. Belonging to the latter group,* Opisthopthalmus capensis *can inflict a very painful sting.*

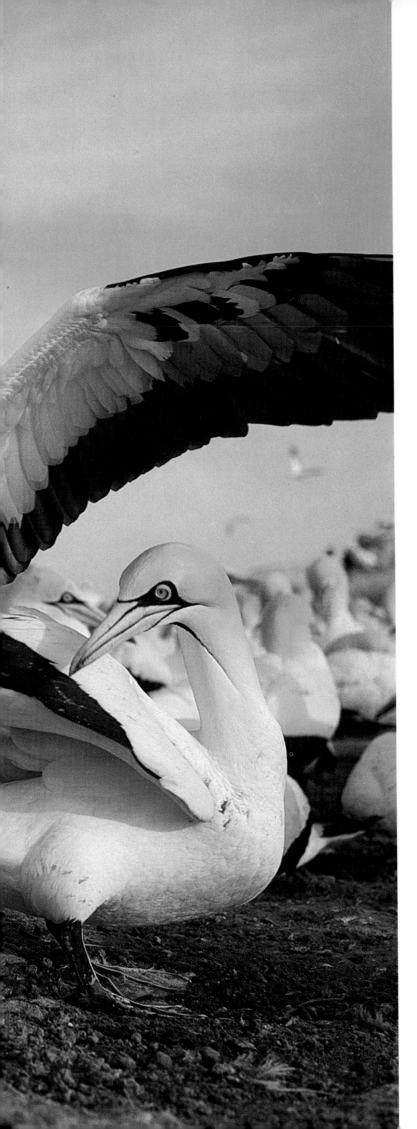

The Coastal Margin

THE INTERFACE BETWEEN LAND AND SEA is an extremely variable and therefore very unstable environment for the organisms which live there. Few species are able to live in conditions which vary so frequently between wet and dry. But for the organisms which are able to exist in these ever-changing conditions, there are many niches in which to fit and a great abundance of energy and nutrients to utilize. Naturally enough, it is easiest for birds to survive here, for they are highly mobile and can easily move from place to place as the need arises, exploiting both land and sea resources as opportunities present themselves. While some birds, such as herons and even seagulls are found not only on the beach but also far inland, others, such as Cape cormorants and black oystercatchers, are found only along the narrow coastal strip.

The intertidal zone is the true meeting place of land and sea, and because of this, it is a highly stressed environment and the limpets, whelks, mussels and algae which live there are both hardy and specialized. Estuaries continue this interface within the terrestrial realm, where tidal and river flows cause a mixing of the two systems in an ever-changing world. It is adaptation to change and the ability to exploit the varying conditions of these habitats that are the most necessary characteristics for organisms that live in estuaries and the intertidal zones.

The Namibian coast is an uncompromising stretch of land, where burning desert meets the chilling upwelled waters of the Atlantic Ocean. There is little evidence of life for mile after mile of sand and sea, but for the cormorants that use the masts of wrecked ships for perches or the few, dense colonies of seals that are packed onto small offshore islands and rocky headlands. The weather-picked rib-cages of long-forgotten ships lie forlornly, locked in their surreal landscapes of shocking blue sea and the mist-draped, golden sand. Many stark wrecks of ships are strewn along the northern section of the Namibian coast, which is aptly called the Skeleton Coast, and it not unusual to find hunger-weakened lions, having found their way to the coast by following dry river beds, scavenging the carcasses of beached whales.

There are 24 known breeding colonies of Cape fur seals (*Arctocephalus pusillus*) on the southern African coast, only four of which are found on the mainland, and two-thirds of this population is to be found along the Namibian coast. The males haul out in mid-October to establish breeding territories in the colonies. Only adult females who come out to pup are allowed access to the colony until all the females have mated. The jet-black pups are born in late November and early December and the breeding females come into oestrus about a week later - when mating begins once again.

While the parents are at sea the pups cluster together densely, but the mothers are able to locate their own pups by using a combination of calls and scent detection. While they lie on the exposed beaches during the day, the pups are easy prey for marauding jackals which stroll through the mainland colonies unchallenged, scavenging placentas and carrying off the helpless, weaker pups.

Left: *Gannets, on Bird Island near Lambert's Bay, have developed intricate displays to defuse territorial aggression in this tightly-packed breeding colony.*

For most of the year the south-east wind blows diagonally across the west coast and Coriolis forces, which are set up by the earth's rotational spinning on its axis, deflect the wind due west away from the coast. This wind pushes a layer of surface water away from the land and to replace it, the cold sub-Antarctic water that flows northwards between South America and Africa wells up along the continental shelf. The intensity of this upwelling, and the related drop in temperature, is a function of how hard and for how long the south-easter blows. When it comes into contact with sunlight, the vast storehouse of nutrients in the upwelled water is made available for the growth of plants and animals that is unequalled anywhere else in the oceans. Plankton proliferates in thick nutrient 'soups' which feed innumerable shoals of anchovies and pilchards and maasbanker, although at times the sudden drop in temperature is so intense that it kills the animals in the area of upwelling.

But while the collective biomass of all living living organisms off the west coast is great, it is made up of relatively few species. On the other side of the sub-continent, the warm Agulhas Current offers a kaleidoscope of shapes and colours of fish and plants, but it has a very low biomass. The generally clear water is indicative of low nutrient concentrations in which few living organisms can be supported - even though sunlight can penetrate much further down

Left: *All of the many small, vegetation-free islands off the south-western coastline are important breeding colonies of marine birds and Sinclair Island, off the southern Namibian 'diamond coast', is an important breeding colony of the Cape cormorant. They have long been the source of guano, the phosphorus-rich bird excreta used as fertilizer.*
Below: *Black-backed jackals of the Namib lead a relatively lazy life, living off the placentas and carcasses of the Cape fur seal.*
Right: *The collecting of penguin eggs by the sailors of old and the recent plundering of the west coast's pelagic fish reserves have had a serious impact on the stability of jackass penguin populations.*

than in the murky waters of the Benguela Current. Most life in the Indian Ocean is concentrated on the coral reefs, where the symbiotic relationship between coral polyps and unicellular algae called zooxanthellae algae begins a food-chain that is the most fascinating and diverse of all marine habitats.

Estuaries and coastal lagoons along the west coast are havens for marine birds, especially the Palaearctic migrants that arrive to spend summer in the southern hemisphere. Migrating waders such as curlews and whimbrels, some of the small plovers and sanderlings, turnstones and sandpipers, greenshanks, godwits and phalaropes congregate in vast flocks at Walvis Bay, Sandwich Harbour, Velorenvlei and Langebaan Lagoon. By international agreement, there are attempts to preserve the habitats of these tireless migrants and to this end large tracts of land in Greenland and Siberia have been declared reserves.

At the mouth of the Langebaan Lagoon lies Saldanha Bay with its numerous islands, which, together with the nearby Bird Island at Lambert's Bay, are all important breeding colonies for sea birds. On Malgas Island in Saldanha Bay and on Bird Island nearly half of the world's Cape Gannets (*Morus capensis*) breed in two tightly packed colonies, where elaborate social and mating rituals are used to avoid conflict. These large diving birds can land vertically but

they need a good run to take off, so runways are established and kept clear by communal consent.

Apart from the significant gannet population, collectively the islands of Saldanha Bay are home to 15 per cent of all the world's crowned cormorants, the largest breeding colony of bank cormorants, 12 per cent of all black oystercatchers, as well as to large colonies of Cape and white-breasted cormorants, sea-gulls and jackass penguins. More than half the world's population of the southern African subspecies of swift tern (*Sterna bergii*) breeds on Marcus Island alone.

What all of these birds have in common is that they feed on pelagic fish, but subsequent to the commercial over-exploitation of this resource the dependent bird populations have been drastically reduced - by up to 95 per cent in the case of the jackass penguin (*Spheniscus demersus*). During the construction of the harbour for the export of iron ore at Saldanha, drastic disruptions were caused to the island breeding sites and large numbers of birds were blown up in blasting operations to deepen the entrance to the bay. Since then a national park has been proclaimed at Langebaan, but the real epilogue to this tale is that the warnings of planners and ecologists have come to pass, with the harbour at Saldanha and the railway to Sishen proving to be an environmental and economic failure.

Our first impression of a sandy beach is that it is a fairly barren place, whereas it is actually one of the most prolific of ecosystems. If measured by the cubic metre, sandy beaches have a greater biomass than any other habitat, made up mainly of small molluscs, isopods and amphipods that feed on washed-up plant detritus, the meiofauna (creatures less than five millimetres long) that live between the sand grains, and bacteria. The waves which bring the food also create a rough, abrasive place in which to live. Most of the creatures within the system are burrowers like the crabs, sand-prawns and snails, which only come out at night or when their holes are under water, so they are seldom seen.

There is a vast circulation of water through sandy beaches and this ensures a continual supply of oxygen and food. Burrowing crea-tures can migrate within the sand to find optimal food and oxygen supplies, while at the same time avoiding predation and desiccation when the tide is out. Sandy beaches have been referred as 'great digestive and incubatory systems', where one flush of water through the sand breaks down 90 per cent of organic matter that is continually being deposited. Given time, a healthy beach will break down even heavy oil slicks, but in many cases the sandy beach fauna has been poisoned by pollution or driven off by beach vehicles, which also compact the sand and starve the system of oxygen.

The familiar plough snails (*Bullia digitalis*) that slide across the beaches at the edge of the surf scavenge on any washed up organic detritus such as dead fish, blue bottles and large medusa jellyfish. Because this food supply is irregular the snails remain inactive for

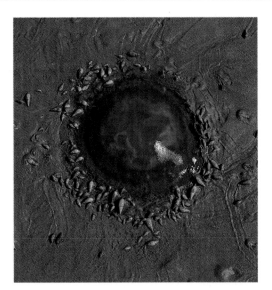

Previous spread: *Cape fur-seals breed on the desert coastline of Namibia, as well as on the islands. Like the jackass penguins, they too have been affected by man's over-utilization of the Atlantic's fish resources.*

Left: *Two species of* Senecio *flowers grow on the coastal dunes of the west coast. These are some of the plants that are hardy enough to withstand salt-laden sea winds and spray. They help to stabilize the dunes, where, under natural conditions of succession, milkwood forests will establish themselves.*

Above: *Plough snails live in large concentrations on sandy beaches, where they are able to migrate up and down the beach as the tide ebbs and flows. In this way they are always close to the dead jellyfish and other sea creatures which the waves offer up and upon which they feed.*

Below: *Greater flamingoes feed on algae and small crustaceans in the Langebaan Lagoon, which is not really a lagoon, but a long narrow inlet with estuarine characteristics.*

weeks at a time, with only the tips of their siphons sticking above water to sample the incoming fare. *Bullia* have an unusually large foot which is used as an underwater sail; waves will deposit the snails to wherever they have dumped food. Because they are at the mercy of water movements, you will not find plough snails where there is a rip current. *Bullia*'s response to food is remarkable and it is especially sensitive to extremely low concentrations of the chemical trimethylamine (a by-product of fish decomposition). Similarly it is repelled by minute concentrations of buterobetaine, which is excreted by their main predators.

Ghost crabs (*Ocypode* spp.) on the east coast show their real strength of numbers on moonlit nights, invading the beaches in scuttling hordes as they search for any edible scraps that the sea has served up during the day. The pale, sand-coloured decapods emerge tentatively from their burrows on the high shore, with eyes held alert on pod-like stalks, and then scurry about with amazing speed in search of any animal food. The crabs also eat isopods and turtle

Above: *Strawberry anemones (Corynactis annulata) are about 1 cm in diameter and often form dense beds such as this one seen here, interspersed with orange sea cucumbers.*
Left: *The beautiful Gorgon's Head or basket star (Astrocladus euryale) is one of the subtidal brittle stars. It feeds by waving its branched arms, filtering tiny particles from the surrounding water.*

Top: *The Cape rock lobster* (Jasus lalandii) *is found on the west coast of southern Africa. This species is exploited commercially, yielding an annual catch of approximately 6 500 tonnes, most of which is exported.*
Left: *Domino fishes* (Dascyllus trimaculatus) *live in close association with several species of sea anemone.*
Below: *The common klipvis* (Clinus superciliosus) *is found on both the west and south coasts of southern Africa.*

hatchlings and will become quite aggressive if threatened, holding their pincers out and jumping towards the intruder.

On the Zululand coast, the ghost crab *O. madagascariensis* dispatches turtle hatchlings as they run the gauntlet from the dunes to the surf. During this time gulls also appear in formation, picking off the struggling baby turtles so that few ever feel the soothing pull of the waves, where they will suddenly be safe from the land predators, but alone in the ocean's immensity. Loggerhead and leatherback turtles lay their eggs on the Maputoland coast of northern Zululand, digging nests in the sand above the high water mark and laying between 500 and 1 000 eggs during the night in mucus-lined repositories. The laying takes place during early summer as the water begins to warm, and the hatchlings emerge in late summer when the water temperature is at a maximum. If the water is late in warming up then laying is delayed accordingly.

Those hatchlings that survive the early hazards of crabs and gulls, and later those of sharks, will drift around in the circulating Agulhas Current for up to three years, living on jellyfish, bluebottles and other related floating organisms. Compared with the rest of the warm and clear Indian Ocean, the Agulhas Current is rich in these floating organisms - as bathers well know. Leatherback turtles (*Dermochelys coriacea*), which breed between Cape Vidal and Sodwana Bay at their only protected breeding site in the world, are the hea-

viest reptiles, weighing up to 650 kilograms when fully grown. The leatherback's nutritional requirements are met almost exclusively by floating hydroids, 95 per cent of whose body mass consists of water.

The rocky shores of the Tsitsikamma and Wild coasts are among the most stressed of marine habitats for animals. The shelled animals that live in the rocky intertidal zones are submerged twice a day in cold water, then they are bashed by waves that on a human scale would be the size of mountains, next they are left high and dry to bake in the sun for about four hours at a time, losing up to 70 per cent of their body fluids before the next pounding begins. Rock pools offer havens that are sheltered from the most powerful wave action and where the inconstant tides are less pronounced. But while the creatures here need less protection from the natural elements, the struggle against predation becomes more intense.

Basket stars or Gorgon's head (*Astrocladus euryale*) are unusual, brittle-stars that are often found clinging to horny corals and sea fans on the bottoms of large pools. They are the fastest-moving echinoderms, having abandoned the tube feet of other starfish. The basket star has repeatedly branching arms that gives it a spectacular appearance, and these are waved around in the water to collect suspended food particles. Boxer crabs (*Lybia*) use a peculiar defence by holding stinging sea-anemones in their claws and thrusting them

towards predatory octopuses and fish, such as the well-camouflaged 'klippies'. The klippies too have to keep a sharp eye out for larger predators such as octopus and rock cod, and so the food-chain continues right up to the large sharks, which compete with crocodiles and man to occupy the tip of life's pyramid in the coastal margin.

Rock pools are decorated by the gaily-coloured shells that are trapped in them, by deep red and blue algae, anemones and luminous nudibranchs which seem to compete to see which one can exhibit the most extravagant array of colours. These small sea-slugs, usually only about five centimetres long, show off their colours as a warning to predators that they are poisonous, for as colouring is used in nature for camouflage, so also it is used as a visible deterrent.

Harmless-looking whelks are among the fiercest predators of the intertidal zone, where they are able to bore through hard shells and devour the molluscs within after dissolving them with sulphuric acid. Where mature whelks of the genus *Burnupena* are found in any numbers there will be no crayfish, and where mature crayfish are found in numbers, whelks will not get a chance to mature. This was demonstrated by a marine zoologist who placed a live crayfish among a colony of *Burnupena* whelks. Very soon, so many whelks had fastened themsleves to the crayfish that it toppled over;

Left: *Red-knobbed coots and yellow-billed ducks feed on aquatic plants and insects in the Serpentine Channel. The Channel connects Bo- and Onder-Langvlei, two coastal lakes of the Wilderness Lakes system. All these lakes were once estuaries which have had their mouths blocked off by the development of coastal dunes. Only Swartvlei retains its identity as an open estuary, but highway, railway and holiday township developments could well seal its fate too.*
Above: *The crab-eating Cape clawless otters are found in marine and fresh waters, from the Western Cape to the Sahara, missing only from the more arid, western areas. Although most often associated with the Tsitsikamma coastline, they are even found in high Drakensberg rivers, up to an altitude of about 2 500 metres.*
Above right: *The kelp gull is no fussy eater, taking live fish, birds eggs and nestlings, as well as offal and human refuse. They are also sometimes called southern black-backed gulls, and are confined to the coast of southern Africa.*

within forty minutes all that was left of the crayfish was an empty carapace.

Among the most fascinating of coastal habitats are the mangrove forests that are found along suitable estuaries from Transkei to Mozambique. The creatures that inhabit mangroves tend to be elusive, as if they know that their habitat is a highly sensitive one. Unfortunately, the most impressive mangroves that once existed in southern Africa were found in places that were also attractive to various industries, such as harbours and factories, especially those in Durban and Richards Bay. Only the few mangrove communities found on the undeveloped Transkei coast, those at remote Kosi Bay in northern Natal and at Maputo Bay in Mozambique survive in a healthy state.

Mangroves are the only estuarine systems that benefit from erosion, as the trees grow by trapping silt in their root networks, slowly spreading out into the water and reclaiming the land. The mangrove trees are unusual in that they grow in the intertidal area where their roots become inundated with saline water and then exposed as the tides ebb and flow. On our eastern tropical and subtropical shores, from the Kobonqaba River mouth to Maputo, are found three types of mangrove trees: the red mangrove (*Rhizophora mucronata*), which has a system of 'prop roots' that protrude out from the main trunk like flying buttresses; the black mangrove (*Bruguiera gymnorrhiza*), which has 'knee roots' that loop in and out of mud like vegetable worms, radiating out from each trunk; and the white mangrove (*Avicennia marina*), which is most common in the southern mangrove communities and has a system of aerial roots, called pneumatophores, which protrude around each tree from the the tacky, oozing substrate like thousands of fingers.

The fruits of the black and red mangroves are heavy, cigar-shaped cylinders that drop into the mud, where they stick and begin to germinate almost immediately. The leaves that fall onto the mud

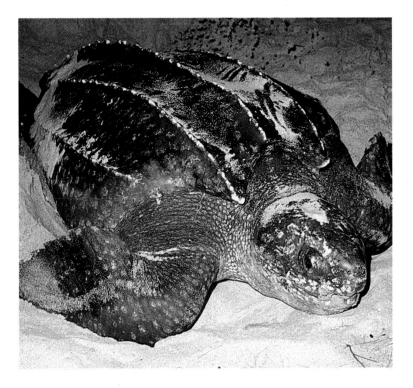

Left: *Transkei's Wild Coast was not so named for its fantastic beauty, its wild seas and rugged shores, but after the 'wild savages' who were encountered here by the survivors of early shipwrecks along this treacherous coast. These survivors underwent arduous journeys and often excruciating hardships on their treks to reach either Cape Town or Lourenço Marques - the only points of civilization established at that time by European colonists and traders.*
Above: *The only breeding site of leatherback turtles on the southern African coast is a protected beach on the Zululand coast. While the adults are often consumed by man, the hatchlings are helpless prey to crabs and gulls, and later small sharks and rays. Few survive to adulthood, when they are due to return to this spot to breed and lay their eggs.*
Right: *Dawn over the Transkei coast - a part of southern Africa's coastal margin that remains relatively unaffected by man's activities.*

into glass-fronted buildings. The generic name for kingfishers refers to a mythological Greek bird that nested on the sea and could calm the waves. Halcyon days are ones of calm and prosperity - an apt description for the sheltered and highly productive environments of these estuaries.

There is no doubt that, despite its enviable splendour, the halcyon days of southern Africa's wild, natural places are past. From its plains have risen large cities; farmlands, suburbs and factories have engulfed its wetlands; its topsoil has been slowly whittled away, gone to silt up and choke its once-prolific estuaries.

Within the next 50 years, the population of southern Africa will probably double. These people will make strong demands on the region's beleaguered natural resources. Fortunately, it seems that, in place of the frontier spirit that reaped without replenishing, a new understanding of nature and its conservation has been awakened. It is no longer considered sufficient merely to protect species of large game, while the natural vegetation is denuded and people starve beyond the borders of national parks.

New conservation strategies include the need to share surplus crops of protected plants and animals in parks and reserves with neighbouring people. In some cases farmers are allowed to graze their cattle under protection within game reserves, in others game is allowed to spread out into rural areas for hunting or farming. Meat, hides and even tusks - the proceeds of culling - help to finance reserves and also the development of local settlements. Subsistence farmers increase their standard of living, the rural poor are employed to help harvest and process these resources, and poacher becomes hunter and protector. While our environment changes, a new balance is being sought between man's needs and the integrity of nature.

at low tide are the main source of food for the many crabs whose burrows can be seen puncturing the area around the mangrove trees. Vividly coloured fiddler crabs (*Uca* spp.), mud-crabs *Sesarma* and the giant mud-crab *Scylla serrata* are the most common mangrove creatures, but they are extremely wary and it takes a great deal of patience to observe and photograph them. They are very sensitive to vibrations and can tell when a leaf lands on the mud at low tide. Then the crabs emerge cautiously from their holes, very slowly at first, and dash out to grab the leaves and drag them back down their holes. Some fiddler crabs, which can be identified by having one pincer much larger than the other, feed by rolling mudballs in their mouths to sift out the detritus. The deposited balls can be seen radiating out from the holes. They also scrape pneumatophores with their pincers for the algae growing on them.

The shy mangrove kingfishers (*Halcyon senegaloides*) eat mainly small crabs and estuarine shrimps and spend most of their time flying about in the mangrove trees. They breed in coastal and riverine forests and, when returning to the coast, these blue, white and grey-black birds with stout red beaks are known to become disorientated in towns and cities, where they kill themselves by flying

Above: *Mangrove swamps are the most productive and yet the most damaged coastal ecosystems in southern Africa. They are estuaries where unusual forest trees grow in the intertidal zone, capturing silt and reclaiming land.*
Right: *The glutinous, richly organic substrate of the mangrove supports an array of unusual life, such as the fiddler crab,* Uca urvillei. *These crabs have an enlarged claw which is used both in territorial and mating displays. They eat the algae on the aerial roots of mangrove trees, leaf litter and well-decayed detritus in the mud, discarding the residue mud in little balls, or pseudofaeces, which decorate the surface of the mud around the bolt-holes of the crabs.*

Further Reading

ACOCKS, J.P.H. 1975. Veld types of South Africa. *Mem. Bot. Surv. S.Afr.* 40: 1-128

ANON. 1980. *Wild flowers of South Africa*. Struik, Cape Town.

BANNISTER, A. & GORDON, R. 1983. *The national parks of South Africa*. Struik, Cape Town.

BANNISTER, A. & JOHNSON, P. 1978. *Namibia, Africa's harsh paradise*. Struik, Cape Town.

BRANCH, G., BRANCH, M. & BANNISTER, A. 1981. *The living shores of southern Africa*. Struik, Cape Town.

BRISTOW, D. & CUBITT, G. 1986. *Okavango*. Struik, Cape Town.

BRISTOW, D. & CUBITT, G. 1986. *Namibia*. Struik, Cape Town.

BRISTOW, D. & WARD, C. 1985. *Mountains of southern Africa*. Struik, Cape Town.

BROWN, L. & FENNESSY, R. 1979. *Birds of the African waterside*. Collins, London.

CLANCEY, P.A. 1985. *The rare birds of southern Africa*. Winchester Press, Johannesburg.

CLARKE, J. & COULSON, D. 1983. *Mountain odyssey in southern Africa*. Macmillan South Africa, Johannesburg.

CLUVER, M.A. 1978. *Fossil reptiles of the South African Karoo*. South African Museum, Cape Town.

COATES PALGRAVE, K. 1983. *Trees of southern Africa*. Struik, Cape Town.

CRAVEN, P. & MARAIS, C. 1986. *Namib flora*. Gamsberg.

CROZE, H. & READER, J. 1977. *Pyramids of life*. Pyramid.

DAVIES, B.R. & DAY, J.A. 1986. *The biology and conservation of South Africa's vanishing waters*. University of Cape Town, Cape Town.

FINCH-DAVIES, C. & KEMP, A. 1982. *The birds of southern Africa*. Winchester Press, Johannesburg.

FUGGLE, R.F. & RABIE, M.A. 1983. *Environmental concerns in South Africa*. Juta, Cape Town.

HAMILTON, G. & COOKE, H. 1954. *Geology for South African students*. CNA, Cape Town.

IRWIN, P., ACKHURST, J. & IRWIN, D. 1980. *A field guide to the Natal Drakensberg*. Wildlife Society of Southern Africa, Durban.

JOHNSON, P. & BANNISTER, A. 1977. *Okavango - sea of land, land of water*. Struik, Cape Town.

KENCH, J. & GERHARDT, K. 1984. *The coast of southern Africa*. Struik, Cape Town.

LEVY, J. 1987. *The complete guide to walks & trails in southern Africa*. Struik, Cape Town.

LOUW, G.N. & SEELY, M.K. 1982. *The ecology of desert organisms*. Longman, London.

MACLEAN, G.L. 1984. *Roberts' birds of southern Africa*. John Voelcker Bird Book Fund, Cape Town.

MEADOWS, M. 1985. *Biogeography and ecosystems of South Africa*. Juta, Cape Town.

MIGDOLL, I. 1987. *Field guide to the butterflies of southern Africa*. Struik, Cape Town.

PATTERSON, R. & BANNISTER, A. 1987. *Reptiles of southern Africa*. Struik, Cape Town.

PEARSE, R.O. 1978. *Mountain splendour - wild flowers of the Drakensberg*. Howard Timmins, Cape Town.

PEARSE, R.O. 1973. *Barrier of spears - drama of the Drakensberg*. Howard Timmins, Cape Town.

ROSS, K. 1987. *Okavango - jewel of the Kalahari*. BBC Books.

RUTHERFORD, M.C. & WESTFALL, R.H. 1986. Biomes of southern Africa - an objective categorization. *Mem. Bot. Surv. S.Afr.* 54:1-98.

SIEGFRIED, W.R. & DAVIES, B.R. 1982. Conservation of ecosystems: theory and practice. *S. Afr. National Scientific Programmes Rep.* 61: 1-97.

SKAIFE, S.H. 1979. *African insect life*. Struik, Cape Town.

SMITHERS, R.H.N. 1983. *The mammals of the Southern African subregion*. University of Pretoria.

STEYN, P. 1982. *Birds of prey of southern Africa*. David Philip, Cape Town.

TRUSWELL, J.F. 1977. *The geological evolution of South Africa*. Purnell, Cape Town.

VOGTS, M. 1982. *South Africa's Proteaceae - know them and grow them*. Struik, Cape Town.

WALKER, C. 1987. *Signs of the wild*. Struik, Cape Town.

WERGER, M.J.A. (ed.) 1978. *Biogeography and ecology of southern Africa*. Vols 1 & 2. W.Junk, The Hague.

Also:

Various issues of *African Wildlife*, the journal of the Wildlife Society of Southern Africa, Linden, Johannesburg.

South African Wildflower Guide series - Botanical Society of South Africa, 1981-85.

Index

Page numbers in bold numerals indicate that the subject is illustrated.